THE COMMON PEOPLE AND POLITICS 1750 – 1790s

Series Editor: Michael Duffy

The other titles in this series are:

THE ENGLISH SATIRICAL PRINT 1600 -1832

The Common People and Politics 1750 – 1790s

by John Brewer

CHADWYCK-HEALEY

CAMBRIDGE

First published 1986

ISBN 0 85964 174 0

Chadwyck-Healey Ltd
Cambridge Place, Cambridge CB2 1NR England

Chadwyck-Healey Inc.
1021 Prince Street, Alexandria, VA 22314 USA

British Library Cataloguing in Publication Data

Brewer, John, 1947–
    The common people and politics, 1750–1890s.—
    (The English satirical print, 1600–1832)
    1. Prints, English.   2. Satire, English—History
    and criticism   3. Politics in art
    I. Title   II. Series
    769′.4932   NE962.P6

Library of Congress Cataloging in Publication Data

Brewer, John, 1947–
    The common people and politics, 1750–1790s.

    (The English satirical print, 1600–1832)
    Bibliography: p.
    1. Great Britain—Politics and government—18th century
    —caricatures and cartoons.   2. English wit and humor,
    Pictorial.   I. Title.   II. Series.
    DA486.B74   1985   769′.49941072   85-6632

Printed by Unwin Brothers Limited, Old Woking, Surrey

CONTENTS

PUBLISHER'S NOTE

In 1978 Chadwyck-Healey published *English Cartoons and Satirical Prints 1320-1832 in the British Museum* in which the 17,000 prints listed in the *Catalogue of Political and Personal Satires* by F. G. Stephens and M. D. George are reproduced on microfilm identified by their catalogue numbers.

British Museum Publications reprinted the Stephens and George catalogue to accompany the microfilm edition and for the first time it became possible for scholars to study the prints that are so exhaustively described in Stephens and George, without needing to visit the Department of Prints and Drawings.

It also made this series possible for it is doubtful whether the seven authors would ever have been able to spend the time in the British Museum necessary to search through this huge collection. As it was they each had access to the microfilm edition which they used for their research.

The reprint of the Stephens and George catalogue is itself now out of print but has been reissued on microfilm by Chadwyck-Healey.

GENERAL EDITOR'S PREFACE

In the course of the seventeenth and eighteenth centuries the English satirical print emerged as a potent vehicle for the expression of political and social opinion. Their development was slow at first, but picking up pace from the 1720s, the prints stood out by the 1780s as the most striking symbol of the freedom of the press in England. Sold usually individually, as works of art as well as of polemic, by the late eighteenth century they constituted the basis of a thriving commercial industry and had established themselves as one of the predominant art forms of the age. The graphic skill of the engraver as well as the pungency of his message makes the English satirical print an immensely attractive, entertaining and very fruitful source for the study of Stuart and Hanoverian England. Surprisingly, although many of the prints survive, this source has been frequently neglected, and it is the aim of this series to remedy that deficiency by showing through the study of selected aspects of the period between 1600 and 1832 how the historian can illuminate the prints and prints can illuminate history. All art forms are the product of particular political and social environments, and this volume together with the rest of the series hopes to set this particular art form – the English satirical print – in its proper historical context by revealing how it gave graphic representation to the ideas, assumptions and environment of that era.

Michael Duffy

PREFACE

This book, like all the volumes in this series, seeks to demonstrate the value of political cartoons to the historian who does not necessarily have visual expertise. It focuses on the topic of the common people and eighteenth-century politics, though many of its arguments are applicable to all political cartoons regardless of their subject matter. Like every scholar in the field I owe an enormous debt to the serried volumes of the *Catalogue of Political and Personal Satires* in the British Museum, which were begun by F. G. Stephens and completed by Dorothy George. It is not a false modesty but a simple description of fact for me to remind the reader that their original catalogue is both far more knowledgeable and far more comprehensive than my own discussion. Those who want a fuller description of the plates in this book are therefore strongly urged to turn to the pages of their catalogue. My text builds on the Stephens/George volume, just as the captions for the prints that I have chosen complement the meticulous remarks of the catalogue entries. I have tried to establish both the visual sources and the visual conventions for the portrayal of the common people in politics in the eighteenth century. Inevitably this has led me to cast my net widely and to include a discussion of the visual archetypes employed to depict the poor and middling sort, even when they were not engaged in politicking. My aim has been to enable the modern reader and viewer to savour the prints in much the same manner as his eighteenth-century counterpart. The text is therefore as much a discussion of eighteenth-century visual mentality or, more accurately, mentalities, as of the cartoons themselves.

I have deliberately chosen not to include a great deal of material by William Hogarth. This is not to deny or belittle Hogarth's importance: he was undoubtedly the most significant English graphic artist of the first half of the eighteenth century, and he accordingly occupies a central place in the introductory discussion. But Hogarth's work, including the famous series of prints – *Marriage a la Mode, The Rake's* and *Harlot's Progress* – is sufficiently familiar for me to have felt entitled to assume that readers are acquainted with most of his prints. Moreover Hogarth's work is so rich and so dense in allusion that it really requires separate and detailed treatment of the kind accorded the artist by Ronald Paulson both in his biography and *catalogue raisonné* of Hogarth's graphic works.

I have incurred many debts in completing this work. Michael Duffy has been both an enthusiastic and patient editor. The staff of the Yale Center for British Art have helped me in many ways, great and small, and provided a stimulating visual environment to which only the most myopic historian could be insensitive. I have greatly benefited from discussions with Ron Paulson and also have to thank him for establishing the group of historians, literary critics and art historians who meet periodically at the Yale Center, and whose comments and criticisms have helped shape the argument of my introduction. Puffin D'Oench, now of Wesleyan University, gave me many valuable leads about the conventions governing the portrayal of different social groups in the eighteenth century. Richard Godfrey and David Alexander have both taught me a good deal about eighteenth-century graphic art in general. The staff of the W. S. Lewis collection in Farmington, Connecticut, especially Mrs Susler, provided me with invaluable aid by placing at my disposal the finest collection of political prints in North America. Joanna Innes, who read the text, helped me with her characteristically unerring criticism. Simon Schama, in his inimitable way, has been an enormous help: his example has shown me that the political and social historian has an important contribution to make to the understanding of graphic art. My greatest debt is to Susan Hewitt. She has read and edited several drafts of the manuscript and made numerous suggestions about presentation and format.

Harvard University   *John Brewer*
1985

INTRODUCTION

'Pictures are made to make seen the unseen.' Jean-Luc Godard.

I.
Low Life and High Art
in Eighteenth-Century England

The portrayal of the common people in eighteenth-century cartoon and caricature seems inextricably associated with two powerful images: John Bull and the sans culottes or Jacobin. Bull was portrayed a stout countryman (usually a yokel) who laboured manfully beneath the burdens of British political life, while the sans culottes, emaciated, fiendish, and with a grin that conveyed both concupiscence and folly, personified the threat of the radical plebeian. Both stereotypes achieved notoriety in the 1790s, the decade of the French Revolution, and their survival at the expense of almost all other images of the common people — apart from those of Hogarth — is largely attributable to the singular genius of James Gillray.

Gillray's vivid and unflattering depictions of a moonfaced, uncomprehending political victim and of the presumptuous, scheming radical have obscured from us earlier and less accomplished portrayals of demotic political figures. Nevertheless, throughout the eighteenth century plebeian politicians found a place in political cartoons and caricatures: engravers depicted them avidly reading the latest news, cheering their candidates on the hustings, taking to the streets to vent their feelings, or vigorously debating political issues in the coffee-house or tavern club.

It would be foolish, however, to suppose that the depiction of popular politicians, much less popular politics, was a major preoccupation of the eighteenth-century cartoonist. Severe restraints, both aesthetic and political, were placed on the portrayal of such *vulgar* subject matter. The plebeian politician was only occasionally depicted — his presence was no more desirable on the copper-plate than in the world of politics itself ; precedence naturally went to his social superiors — and when his portrayal was inescapable, his conduct was usually either censured or made the subject of a sententious story. Gillray's attitude — that the plebs were either politically passive, the worthy object of condescending sympathy in the light of their misfortunes, or were active and radical, thereby brutally violating the natural political order — was a view which, if it was not expressed by other engravers with as much skill and ferocity, nevertheless commanded widespread support throughout the century. There is, therefore, a striking parallel between the attitudes towards popular politics expressed by the political cartoonist and the mixture of self-righteousness and alarm with which gentlemen greeted the political interests of the plebs.

It is tempting to push this type of analogy further — to argue that the cartoons reflect not only patrician *attitudes* towards popular politics but provide us with an image of the phenomenon itself. Seen in this light the rise and progress of popular politics is mirrored by the increasing importance in the prints of the plebeian politician: he begins off-stage, becomes part of the mise-en-scène, and is eventually cast as protagonist. We can

15

chronicle this move out of the wings and into the limelight. The aristocratic Whig supremacy of Walpole produced relatively few depictions of popular political activity; the popular appeal of the elder Pitt and the emergence of radicalism in the 1760s spawned an increasing number of cartoons that took popular politics as their subject matter; and, in the age of the American and French Revolutions, the common man, whether patriot or radical, excited the obsessive attention of Gillray and his colleagues.

The idea that the political print reproduces or accurately reflects the state of politics and the position of the common man is superficially very attractive. For many of us there is a ring of truth to the proposition that images mirror society. The argument, like many platitudes, has a gratifying simplicity: there clearly is a sense in which political cartoons inform us about the character of politics. But the image – the print that was boldly displayed in the shops of Matthew Darly, Mrs Humphrey and Thomas Tegg – cannot be seen simply as a window through which we can peer in order to observe the character of eighteenth-century political life. The interpretation of political cartoons is altogether more intractable and complex.

The assumption that political prints provide an unrefracted image of political life produces its own distortions. Its most egregious error is to presuppose what it seeks to find – the meaning of the cartoon or caricature is prejudged. To take a print of an eighteenth-century crowd such as that in Plate *1**, for example, and use it as the basis for an analysis of the eighteenth-century 'mob' is to assume that the engraver employs only one convention, that of 'realism'. Yet, as we shall see, the figures in the crowd and their formal arrangement owe as much to a stock of visual stereotypes derived from other sources as they do to a desire to record the types of people present.

Secondly the assumption of realism is usually accompanied by a strong tendency to divorce the medium from the message: technique, method, graphic convention are all thrust aside in pursuit of content and subject matter. In consequence all sense of what is distinctive and remarkable about this type of *visual* evidence is lost – we might as well be reading a pamphlet or newspaper as examining a cartoon. Implicit in this approach, therefore, is the assumption that visual materials cannot offer us insights that are not obtainable elsewhere. What we have, in other words, is a form of iconoclasm – the destruction of images by their treatment as *non-visual* forms of evidence. This trivialisation of the most perspicuous quality of cartoons – that they are graphic art – not only creates an artificial distinction between means and ends but also prevents us from seeing the prints *historically*, from grasping their meaning and significance for an eighteenth-century audience. Much of the success of the eighteenth-century political print stemmed from its use of a visual vocabulary and of visual convention whose rich allusiveness was savoured by its viewers. The historian cannot appreciate what many prints meant to their eighteenth-century audience or audiences – he cannot see them through eighteenth-century eyes – unless he understands the visual and perceptual conventions of that day.

*Italicised numbers in the text refer to the plates in this volume. Numbers prefixed with BMC refer to catalogue numbers in the British Museum *Catalogue of Political and Personal Satires.*

In the eighteenth century the representation of the political world of the humble was bound by the same rules and conventions that governed the portrayal of nearly every aspect of 'low life'. Originally restricted and circumscribed, the visual vocabulary used to depict demotic life grew by leaps and bounds during the course of the century. By the outbreak of the French Revolution, the era that saw the prime of Rowlandson and Gillray, a variety of stock characters and situations, popular genres, symbols and associations had become well established. They were well tried and much trusted weapons in what Gombrich has felicitously described as 'the cartoonist's armoury'.[1]

The development of these visual conventions was a slow and painstaking process. Before the age of Hogarth, prints of plebeian life (such as they were) shared the constraints that limited the English print business as a whole. In the early eighteenth century the tradition of English visual representation, especially of English painting, was like a sickly adolescent, neither healthy nor mature. Moreover, English art was overwhelmingly dominated by its imperious relations on the European continent who could boast not only an excellent aesthetic pedigree but a degree of refinement not found among their callow English cousins. Even in the relatively humble sphere of engraving, the French and, to a lesser extent, the Dutch dominated. There were few competent English line engravers; a European apprenticeship or training was at a premium. A clear pecking order existed in the print trade: the continentals were employed for the most prestigious and technically demanding tasks – reproducing old masters, for example – while the majority of English engravers were consigned the hack work, producing trade cards, bill heads, share certificates, bank notes and theatre tickets. The engraver of political prints, whether European or British – and he might be either – occupied a position somewhere between these two extremes.[2]

European aesthetic imperialism, emanating from Paris and Rome, not only affected the structure of the English print trade but prescribed rigorous canons of taste. History painting, especially the portrayal of classical antiquity, constituted the highest and most edifying form of art, the sort of work that the connoisseur would be delighted to hang in his cabinet. Portraiture and landscape were further down the aesthetic hierarchy, while *genre*, the depiction of everyday life, marked the lowest form of expression to which the artist could descend. Fine art and low life should not mix: the humble, who by definition were not heroic, were an insufficiently exalted subject for the great painter. This hierarchy of values is well brought out in Thornhill's dilemma when he was commissioned to paint George I's landing in England for Greenwich hospital: 'there was a vast crowd which to represent would be ugly, and not to represent would be false'.[3]

Though such aesthetic rules were less strictly adhered to in engraving than in painting, they were sufficiently powerful both to constrict the development of an idiom with which to depict the common people and, when it did emerge, to affect the form that it took. Though continental canons of taste came under fire from British artists – most notably from Hogarth who carried on a crusade to establish an English school of painting and the respectability of portraying 'low life' – the patrician attitudes that they embodied proved remarkably enduring. It is surprising, for example, how frequently plebeians were omitted from scenes in which we would naturally expect their presence. Many of the early crowds in political cartoons consist entirely of gentlemen – there is not a prole in sight. Even Gillray, two generations later, was more likely to portray Fox, Sheridan and Lansdowne as Jacobins than to depict the plebeians themselves (e.g. 2). And as late as 1806 William Ward's mezzotint of George Morland's Alehouse Politicians was condemned as 'too low a subject to merit the same attention as several other pictures of this artist, who gave himself such a latitude upon some occasions, that was very disgusting to an eye of taste'.[4]

By the early nineteenth century the objection to Ward's print of Morland's painting was less to the subject matter than to the manner in which it was portrayed. After Hogarth the common people were a popular subject for the engraver, but the same aesthetic conventions that had earlier relegated the plebs to pictorial obscurity now required that they be shown either as comic and grotesque, especially when they acted in an unrefined or socially inappropriate manner, or as worthy, deserving and industrious (an indication that they knew their station). The portrayal might be jocose, sentimental or picturesque but it was rarely at all realistic. Ward and Morland's crime (and, as we shall see, they committed an unusual offence) was to show humble men drinking and politicking – clear signs that these plebs were neither industrious nor deserving – without making them appear comic, foolish or, in Gillray's manner, palpably satanic.

Aesthetic dicta, and the socially discriminatory assumptions on which they were based, inhibited the cartoonist who portrayed the common people politicking. In the early years of the eighteenth century, he could draw very little from the traditions of 'high art' to develop a visual language of the plebs. Admittedly a number of mezzotints of Dutch *genre* paintings of the seventeenth century provided some inspiration (they can be seen reflected in Hogarth's work, for example) but overall the printmaker had to turn elsewhere – away from the top end of the market and the continental artist and towards the mundane world of the English craftsman. Book illustration, English woodcuts of the street cries of London, trade cards and shop signs rather than grand canvases provided the printmaker with his visual sources. The engraver of the trade card, like the painter of the shop sign, was freed of the aesthetic constraints of 'high art' and virtually impelled by the nature of his task – to produce an informative advertisement – to embrace subject matter that would have made the history painter shudder. The trade card and the shop sign often depicted ordinary men going about their daily business. Ambrose Heal's famous selection of eighteenth-century trade cards, for example, includes illustrations of humble men and women serving behind the shop counter, calico printing, working letter and copper-plate presses, blowing glass, loading coal, emptying privies, lighting lamps, sweeping chimneys and collecting 'night soil'.[5] All of these activities are portrayed in a matter-of-fact manner to provide the potential customer with a clear indication of the goods and services offered. They were not, it scarcely needs to be added, the subject matter of great art.

Book illustration seems to have offered a similar opportunity for the engraver to flout continental convention. Most of the earliest eighteenth-century depictions of the common people in the British Museum collection come not from separately published prints but from books. This applies not only to illustrations for Samuel Butler's *Hudibras* with their robust and sinewy demotic figures (eg. *3, 4*) but to the stylised depiction of a street scene with an itinerant seller of nuts (*5*), the working shoemaker, 'Crispin Cobler', who graced the frontispiece of a publication of 1709 (6), and the motley crew of electors found between the covers of a shilling pamphlet, *The Humours of a Country Election*, that appeared in 1734 (7). Hogarth's biographer, Ronald Paulson, has justly remarked,

> *English book illustration of the first half of the eighteenth century (probably from 1720 on) contributed strongly to the trend away from portraiture, even from idealised history painting, toward treatment of everyday subjects. Picaresque tales and other forerunners of the English novel . . . served as important transitional agencies, providing artists like Hogarth and Vanderbank with a subject and (in book illustrations) an outlet for concerns that were suppressed by orthodox critical standards.[6]*

Although the engravers of prints of the common people turned to vernacular forms derived from popular and commercial illustration, they never entirely rejected the canons of 'good taste'. The depiction of demotic taste was therefore a synthesis of two traditions, one derived from the conventions of 'high art' and the other from much more mundane forms of expression. Used by an imaginative and creative artist, the tension between the two forms could be exploited to brilliant effect; such, of course, was the achievement of Hogarth in his comic, history painting. His innovative and provocative work sought to elevate everyday subject matter to the realm of high art. At a more mundane level the engraver of political cartoons could use the technique of anomalous juxtaposition – depicting a pleb like a classical hero (8) or an aristocrat like a figure from a trade card (a favourite device for the portrayal of Charles James Fox) – in order to convey a telling political message.

This intermingling of traditions and conventions provided the cartoonist both with a distinctive idiom in which to convey the *mores* of the common people and with a series of characteristic genres and situations for the depiction of popular politics. Before, therefore, we go on to consider the changing character of representations of plebeian politics, especially as they developed in the three distinctive periods of the 1750s and 60s, the 1780s, and the 1790s, we need to examine the stereotypes and genre that persisted throughout the period.

II.

Physiognomy, Deportment and Dress:
the Visual Language of Social Convention

What were the conventions that enabled the viewer of an eighteenth-century print to recognize the common man? Throughout the eighteenth century engravers employed two standard devices: the first relied on the depiction of physiognomy and body language to reveal a person's class; the second, and perhaps more obvious, technique was to use costume – especially working costume – together with the tools of a person's trade to show his humble station.

The conventions governing the depiction of physical appearance were largely derived from the works of two highly influential figures: Charles Le Brun, a French academician who wrote the standard work on physiognomy, gesture and the 'picturing of the passions', and Gerard de Lairesse, the author of a widely disseminated painting manual, *The Art of Painting in all its Branches*.[7] Their work embodied two crucial assumptions: they took it for granted that the appearance of the face and body not only revealed sentiments but also character (what we, perhaps, would call personality), and that different sorts of posture and stance – body language – were associated with different social groups.

In almost all of the cartoons that portray common people, the plebs are depicted with ungracious, ill-formed features on a face whose conformation is exaggerated by a variety of crude expressions. *St Monday* (9), the frontispiece to a work on low life, depicts several labourers and tradesmen taking Monday as a holiday – hence *Saint Monday* – rather than devoting themselves to work. They all, without exception, have the coarse features of the (indolent) common man. The contrast with gentlemen is an explicit one: the humble ogle, leer and stare, they do not merely look; their open-mouthed credulity indicates both their low social standing and their lack of refinement and intelligence. Thus in *Doctor Rock's Political Speech to the Mob in Covent Garden* (10), the quack addresses a crowd that includes a man on the left with a shaven head whose expression – indeed, whose whole posture – speaks of plebeian gullibility. This gaping, credulous look is frequently reiterated in the political prints: the blacksmith in *The Blacksmith lets his Iron grow cold attending to the Taylor's News* (11), for example, resembles Doctor Rock's auditor – he has the same unashamed stare and similarly thrusts his head forward (in a manner that Lairesse saw as archetypal of his class)[8] in an effort to comprehend matters that the print quite clearly implies are far beyond his limited comprehension.

If not credulous, the poor were portrayed as comic: 'clownishness', Lairesse decreed, 'must appear in them'.[9] The plebeian found in engravings did not smile politely; he laughed and guffawed, opening his mouth and exposing his teeth. As one print (12) put it, 'The rabble gather round the Man of News/*And listen with their*

21

mouths' (my italics). Such vapid grins and grimaces, which can be seen for example, on the news vendor's face in *Stand Coachman, or the Haughty Lady well Fitted (13)* or on almost all of the plebs attending the effigy-burning in Plate *1*, were, from a genteel point of view, contemptible, preposterous and risible. For, as one eighteenth-century conduct manual stressed, 'it is not becoming to break out into violent loud laughter upon any occasion whatsoever, and worse to laugh always, without any occasion, like a country Milk-Maid'.[10] Notice here the explicit association of a socially undesirable type of conduct with the characteristic behaviour of a member of the labouring poor.

The practice of linking social groups and types of conduct embraced not only facial expressions but carriage and deportment. Most eighteenth-century conduct manuals – and there were a good many of them – aspired 'to assist the Body and Limbs with Attitudes and Motions easy, free and graceful, and thereby distinguish the polite gentleman from the rude rustic',[11] or, as one guide which did not mince words put it, they prevented a man from 'turning in his Toes like the Master of a Ship, and tossing his Arms up and Down like a Fire Office Porter'.[12] Lairesse transposed these prescriptions into his rules for representation. An erect carriage, out-turned feet and elegantly placed hands were, he considered, the natural appurtenances of the genteel and therefore the logical means by which they were identified. Plebs, on the other hand, were pigeon-toed, stooped and leant forward, never knew where to place their hands and assumed awkward and deformed postures. In the unlikely eventuality that the aspiring painter or draftsman failed to comprehend his dicta, Lairesse provided diagrams and drawings distinguishing the classes by their respective body language.[13]

The convention linking deportment and class was regularly used in political and social prints. One of the most distinguished instances of its use can be found in the first scene of Hogarth's *Marriage a la Mode (14)*. The aristocratic groom-to-be, although thoughtless and vain, sits in exemplary fashion, his knees apart and feet pointing outwards. (If the reader thinks this pose natural, he should try sitting in such a manner.) His future father-in-law, a city merchant, lacks these graces: he sits with his knees together and feet parallel, peering-forward. His daughter – admittedly angered by the marriage transaction – also lacks the patrician finesse that is evident in *her* future father-in-law who, despite his gout, sits with an appropriately dignified and erect carriage. Social distinctions are expressed through the nuances of body language.[14]

This technique appears frequently in political cartoons, although its application is usually much cruder and less subtle than in Hogarth's work. A characteristic example is the print of *The Robin Hood Society (15)*. The members of this famous debating club of London tradesmen and mechanics are so awkwardly composed that one is led to suspect graphic incompetence. But the composition of the figures, especially of two seated men in the centre, is undoubtedly intended to convey their complete lack of social grace and therefore their relatively humble social origin.

The practice of identifying men's class and character by their physiognomy was not confined to the small group familiar with the canons of academic painting. Indeed a very large audience would have understood the implications of the *way* in which figures in political cartoons were portrayed. Physiognomic assumptions were assimilated not only by the gentleman collector but by the aspiring bourgeoisie who wished to know how to stand, how to look, and how to comport themselves. This was the audience that George Alexander Stevens, a failed actor and notorious perpetrator of practical jokes, appealed to in his *Lecture on Heads*. Originally performed at the Haymarket in 1764, the lecture toured the English provinces, where it was enormously successful with its audience of local gentry, merchants and bourgeoisie, and then went to the American colonies where it was especially well received in Boston and Philadelphia. Stevens displayed a series of heads (they can be seen in *16*, the frontispiece to the printed version of the lecture) which represented both different social types and different characters. His accompanying patter was both in the manner of the head displayed and a commentary on the social type. The objects of Stevens' satire included 'the broad grinner' – a demotic fool – a Frenchman, a Spaniard and a Dutchman, opera singers, London 'bloods', feminists, and humble politicians. His commentary on 'a Politician and City Epicure', no. 46 in *16*, is typical:

> *This head is a representation of one of many thousands, which swarm in and about this metropolis, whose whole time is taken up between the affairs of state and the affairs of the kitchen. He was a great lover of politics and venison . . . He would no more miss a mail than he would a venison feast; but would hover over a newspaper for battles and slaughters, like a vulture over its prey; and thought soldiers and sailors were only made to be knocked on the head, for him to read all about it in the newspaper. – He constantly read every political pamphlet, that came out on both sides of the question, and agreed with the author which he read last.*[15]

Stevens' droll spectacle, which remained popular into the nineteenth century, had an explicitly didactic purpose: to teach propriety and proper conduct by satirising the gaucheries of the socially maladroit.[16]

At this point some historians, especially those who pride themselves on their commonsensical approach to historical problems, will probably object that we are complicating what is actually a very simple issue. According to this argument patricians and plebeians are identified by feature and posture in cartoons because this visual distinction was obvious in everyday life. Gentlemen, having read their conduct manuals and attended to the strictures of their dancing masters, really did deport themselves with an erect carriage and outwardly pointing toes; equally the humble had not learnt the social restraint that prevented them from slouching, staring and contorting both their bodies and features.

This is, of course, a variant of the case for visual realism that I have already criticised. Though there is doubtless some truth to this argument it misses one essential point: that physiognomy and deportment were used by the cartoonist not only to describe but to praise or condemn. If, for example, we place Robert Dighton's *Court of Equity or a Convivial City Meeting* (*17*) beside *The Robin Hood Society* (*15*) we can observe this normative use of physical appearance. The two prints depict men of the same class: they are tradesmen and small masters, members of the middling sort. The

23

Robin Hood Society includes parish schoolmasters, apothecaries, shoemakers and a baker for a president, while Dighton's convivial meeting is attended by a distiller, a printer's clerk (holding a copy of the *Morning Chronicle*), a silver smith, a publican, a sausage-maker and a bricklayer, as well as by the artist himself. One would expect two groups with such similar social backgrounds to be depicted in the same manner. The prints, however, portray what appear to be markedly different social worlds. Members of the Robin Hood Society have broad foolish-looking grins, but in the other group there is not even a flicker of a smile. Posture is similarly contrasted: the debaters in Plate *15* stand and sit in the most awkward, angular (and therefore vulgar) fashion; Dighton's citizenry, on the other hand, appear poised, conveying an easy dignity that verges on elegance. Indeed, the pose of Mr. Towse, the full-length figure on the right, could have been taken directly from an eighteenth-century conduct book.

Clearly the engraver's purpose in *The Robin Hood Society* is to place the debating club in the worst possible light. Physiognomy is used to deride the tradesmen. This hostility stems, no doubt, from the socially undesirable character of the club's activities. According to another print (*18*), members of the Robin Hood 'associate together in an illegal Manner to ridicule Religion, scoff at Morality, rail at the Ministry, and bid defiance to all Things Sacred and Divine'. Such a violation of the proprieties of good conduct was given *visual* expression in the misshapen form and features of the debaters. The print, like Stevens' *Lecture on Heads*, has a dual purpose: to entertain — we laugh at the presumptuous folly of the tradesmen; and to instruct — we learn through ridicule and satire to draw the line between acceptable and undesirable behaviour.

Dighton could have made an equally sententious point in the *Court of Equity*. A number of the tradesmen in his print had been intimately connected with radical politics in London. The tavern that forms the venue of the 'convivial meeting', the Globe in Fleet Street, was one of several centres of Wilkite activity in the 1760s and 1770s, and its proprietor, Thomas Thorpe, who is seen carrying a punchbowl, was a personal friend of Wilkes, as well as a Common Councilman for Farringdon Without, where he was elected on a radical ticket. Hurford and Thorn, also portrayed, were strong Wilkes supporters. Dighton might, therefore, have chosen to give his citizens a physiognomy suitable to their (somewhat disreputable) political reputations. Perhaps he was sympathetic to their politics: he does, after all, appear in the print and was a member of the convivial society of the Globe. Perhaps the engraving was produced for radical sympathisers, or possibly it reflects the new-found respectability of a different sort of politics. Whatever the explanation, the dignity that Dighton imparts to these London citizens (and therefore the approval that he expresses) represents the other, more beneficent face of the physiognomic conventions employed so critically in *The Robin Hood Society*.

Both Dighton and the engraver of *The Robin Hood Society* employ the other chief convention used to depict eighteenth-century tradesmen and labourers, namely the use of costume or the tools of a trade to indicate a person's occupation. Dighton's

24

allusions are subtle: Thorpe, the publican, carries a punchbowl, a symbol of the tavern keeper's calling, while Hamilton, the printer's clerk, grasps the latest number of the *Morning Chronicle*; there is nothing forced or artificial in this situation, for the newspaper and the punchbowl are objects that an eighteenth-century audience would expect to see in a convivial tavern setting. But in *The Robin Hood Society* trade credentials intrude awkwardly upon the scene. The loaf of bread that mysteriously hangs like a sword of Damocles above the head of the baker and the shoemaker's last that juts out from beneath the arm of one of the standing figures serve to remind us of the other world that the members of the debating society inhabit. These men, we are being told, pose as learned rhetoricians, but their true vocation – and one that they are currently neglecting for the thrills of disputation – is at the shop-counter or in the workplace.

The convention that associated a particular item of dress or a special tool with a specific trade provided engravers with a visual shorthand with which to describe tradesmen and labourers. The trades that most frequently appeared were the most comprehensively described. The butcher who can be seen in the left background of *The Robin Hood Society* is identified by his large apron and the steel that hangs from his waist. In other prints butchers are depicted with candles in their hats – used to light the cellars in which they stored their meat; more often they were shown gripping meat cleavers with which they beat marrow bones to make 'rough music' on such festive and riotous occasions as the Lord Mayor's Day (*19*) or the celebration of the Peace of Aix-la-Chapelle (*20*). The chimney sweep or climbing boy appear in the cartoons almost as frequently as the butcher. Squat and sooty, and often in silhouette, he waves his handbrush or his pan; by the end of the century we can also see, especially in Gillray's work, the metal hat-badge that sweeps were required to wear as a result of Jonas Hanway's legislation (e.g. *21*). The depiction of most trades, however, depended on simple metonymy. Each trade had its sign just as each shop had its signboard. Tailors were identified by their scissors, hairdressers and barbers by their comb and wig-box, sailors by their striped trousers, the lamplighter by his ladder and oil lamp, and the ballad singer by the sheaves of printed songs she carried over her arm. The coalheavers who unloaded Newcastle coals on London's wharfs were distinguished by their curious leather hats; the yoke with its two pails identified the pretty milkmaid doing her daily rounds; maidservants had caps and mops, carters and draymen carried whips, fruitsellers pushed wheelbarrows or carried panniers, and the knife-grinder could be spotted by his revolving grindstone.

The Politicians (*22*), a print of 1763 that satirises the intense interest in politics in the early years of George III's reign, portrays many of these occupational figures. They include (moving from left to right) a porter with his load, a milkman (rather than the usual milkmaid), a carter carrying a whip and reading a newspaper, a ragged ballad singer, a blacksmith with tongs, a cobbler holding shoes, a butcher, a tailor, a barber carrying a wig-box, a pot-boy and a lamplighter. All are deeply embroiled in political controversy.

It is unusual to find so many occupations in a single print, but their mise-en-scène is typical. Labourers and tradesmen, when not at the workbench or in the tavern, were usually shown in the open street. This largely reflects the widely held belief that the street, in Henry Fielding's words, was 'the absolute right of the mob'.[17] The rule of the multitude prevailed: aristocrats in court dress had their rich clothes bespattered with mud, foreigners were mocked and reviled, pickpockets punished by mobbing or ducking, and disputes settled through popular arbitration. 'Out of doors' was open, 'democratic', space; indoors, the world of aristocracy and oligarchy prevailed. And if the caricaturist wished to contrast 'high' and 'low' politics, he often portrayed the former in an enclosed space and the latter in the open air (eg. 23). The two realms are separated spatially *and* depicted in different sorts of space. Occasionally, however, they overlapped: the rich preserved their sense of exclusiveness in the form of the private coach and the sedan chair, both of which enclosed public space, reasserting oligarchy and privilege in the egalitarian atmosphere of the public thoroughfare. The tension between 'open' and 'closed' space, between equality and hierarchy, is well brought out in *Stand Coachman, or the Haughty Lady well Fitted* (13) in which 'street people' treat an arrogant aristocrat's coach as a public right of way.

Such instances of mob rule were possible because the eighteenth-century street, especially the London street, was so crowded. Tradesmen, hawkers and street sellers wandered through lanes, courts and alleys, vociferously crying their wares and loudly offering their services. These cacophonous street cries which, as Addison remarked, astonished the foreigner and frightened the visiting country squire,[18] had long been the subject of a literary and visual genre. Descriptions of 'The Cries of London' date back at least to the fifteenth century. They originally appeared as broadsheets and ballads or in pamphlet form. Like the trade card, they were a popular narrative source that had not previously attracted the sophisticated artist and engraver. During the eighteenth century, however, the Cries were both widely disseminated and taken up by artists of stature. They appeared on silver counters and tokens, as a deck of playing cards and in children's literature; numerous editions of the Cries were either painted or engraved. Lauron's late seventeenth-century series, probably the most popular in the first half of the eighteenth century, went through three editions in 1687–8, and reappeared thereafter in 1688–9, 1709, 1711, 1731, 1733 and 1750. Other series produced by Sandby, Rowlandson and Francis Wheatley were all a commercial success.[19]

Artists and engravers used the Cries in their own distinctive ways. Rowlandson, for example, employed the genre to develop variations on his favourite theme of sexual relations between men and women (24–8), while Wheatley sentimentalised the poor — his female street sellers comport themselves like ladies of high fashion and walk streets that are as clean and uncluttered as a ballroom floor. But all these variations, whether elegant, picturesque or comic, drew on a stock set of characters. Similarly, when political cartoonists depicted a street scene with a sweep, a butcher or a fruitseller, they were drawing on a genre that was readily recognisable to their audience.

26

III.

Visual Themes in the
Portrayal of Popular Politics

1. POPULAR POLITICS AS DISORDER, 1760–80

Political cartoonists had, therefore, a variety of sources, conventions and traditions on which they could draw: they had a visual language with which to depict plebeian politics. What then did they say? What were the chief themes of political caricature and how did they develop over time? The different motifs and perspectives employed by engravers to depict the common people do not fit snugly into a tidy temporal scheme. We can, however, make a number of broad generalisations.

First and foremost there is very little depiction of or response to popular politics before the 1750s. This is sometimes explained by the predominance of the emblematic print in the period before the accession of George III. This type of print, it is argued, did not lend itself to such 'realistic' and humble subject matter. But prior to 1750 considerable progress had been made in the elaboration of conventions and genre for the depiction of many aspects of demotic life *apart* from politics. Street crowd scenes, for example, had become quite numerous, though they usually depicted *social* events such as the discharge of insolvent debtors (*29*), a Fleet wedding (*30*), the celebration of Boxing Day (*31*), a drunken frolic in Covent Garden (*32*), holiday junketings on Greenwich Hill (*33*), or the flight from the City during the earthquake panic of 1750 (*34*). The political crowd, apart from a few prints of London elections in 1747 (*35–7*) had to await the Wilkite era.

Indeed there can be very little doubt that the political excitement of the late 1750s and 1760s played a major role in bringing the plebeian politician within the purview of the satirical print. The early years of George III's reign saw the development of nearly all of the genres depicting popular politics that were to endure into the nineteenth century. Broadly speaking the portrayal of popular politics falls into three categories. The first is the depiction of plebeian politics as a form of disorder. This includes not only the political riot but tavern and coffee-house scenes (e.g. *38, 39*) where emphasis is placed on the divisive and contentious character of political debate. In all of these scenes there are vivid signs of entropy. Ramshackle buildings, unkempt rooms, dishevelled dress – whether a threadbare coat, untied breeches, wrinkled, falling-down stockings or a cockeyed wig – the spilled drink, glasses tumbling from a table, an upturned punchbowl, the collapsing table or overturned pannier of fruit, the unattended dog, defecating on clothes, urinating on men's legs, destroying cloth or slyly pilfering a piece of meat: they all help convey the disorderliness of popular politics (e.g. *40–3, 12, 44–7*).

An Election Entertainment at Brentford (*42*) published in December 1768 during the electoral contest for Middlesex between the Wilkite, John Glynn, and the courtier, Sir Beauchamp Proctor, is a characteristic example of this genre. The print depicts the usual electoral vices – the two seated figures in the foreground are both being offered bribes: one, a butcher (recognisable by the steel that hangs from his waist) refuses while the other, gnawing a bone (as does the dog at his feet) accepts. (Notice, incidentally, the fashionable poise of the butcher as contrasted with the vulgar posture and gross demeanour of the gentleman accepting the bribe.) Signs of disorder abound. On the left, the tap boy or waiter carrying a roast is so distracted by the proceedings that he spills the gravy from the joint; the bribe leads to an overturned punchbowl and wine bottle. On the floor a large pug gnaws a marrow bone while on a chair to the right a cat chews what appears to be a drumstick. A ragged and drunken elector in the background is so carried away by his enthusiasm for Glynn that he spills his tankard of ale on an equally dishevelled character who is picking the pocket of the man seeking to bribe the butcher. And finally, to the far right, in a scene that combines lasciviousness with depravity, a serving wench is having her pocket picked as she and a man embrace. The visual message is clear: politics, especially demotic or radical politics, not only encourages disorder and licentiousness – men like the tap boy neglect their jobs, are crapulous like Glynn's ragged supporter, or blatantly dishonest like the bribed elector or the pickpocket – popular politics *is* a form of disorder, like a collective malady or madness. (This, of course, was a theme that Gillray took up with a vengeance in the 1790s.)

An Election Entertainment also employs one other widely-used device to convey a sense of disorderliness. Unlike most of the cartoons that depict the leaders of the political nation, this print's subject matter is not entirely contained within the framework of the engraving. The activity that the viewer sees – the carousing, bribing, politicking and wenching – clearly extends beyond the boundaries of the composition. The sense of rude, undirected energy is expressed visually by the boisterous democratic group which is crammed within the print – there is a high degree of *compression* here – but which also bursts out of the picture's frame.

This device, visualising a lack of containment or restraint, was occasionally used in such interior scenes as the Brentford electoral treat; more commonly, however, it was employed to depict the irresistible force of the mob. Prints of a fracas during the Middlesex election of December 1768 (*41*), a riot involving the Lord Mayor outside London's Mansion House (*40*), two confrontations between Wilkites and courtiers at the City's Temple Bar (*48*) and outside St. James' Palace (*49*), a radical procession marching effigies of ministers to Tower Hill (*50*), and of the wild and turbulent scenes that accompanied the plundering and destruction of Newgate prison during the Gordon Riots of 1780 (*51–3*) all portray the crowd, regardless of its degree of internal cohesion or discipline, as an unbridled body that *trespasses* both beyond customary social restraint and beyond the viewer's field of vision. Eighteenth-century engravers show that they share Elias Canetti's sense of the crowd's capacity to cross customary boundaries and to change the shape of both social and pictorial space.[20] The intensity of these crowd scenes

28

varies according to the degree of violence depicted, but in all the prints there is a sense of foreboding: the crowd looms large, as if it would engulf all around it.

Plebeian crowds were only one instance of popular political initiative. Demotic politics, as they appeared in the cartoons, also included newspaper reading, debating in taverns and ale-houses, and participation in the electoral process. All of these activities were usually portrayed through one of three genres, each of which corresponds to a particular historical moment in the development of popular politics. From the 1750s to the 1770s it was most common to portray popular political initiative as yet another instance of a general social phenomenon, the emulation of the rich by the poor. The second genre dominated the cartoons of the 1780s. Social emulation was replaced by social dialogue: patricians and plebeians were anomalously juxtaposed, condemning not only popular politics but the willingness of certain genteel politicians – most notably the followers of Charles James Fox – to encourage demotic political participation. Finally, the era of the French revolution transformed the comic, socially maladroit and usually risible efforts of the common people into a grotesque, even satanic attack on the natural order of political society.

Each of these temporal phases also produced archetypes of the true plebeian Englishman. Between c. 1750 and 1780 he was robust and tough, a hale and hearty figure, personified by a sailor or butcher, and overtly contrasted to the emaciated and scabrous Scot, or the mincing, effeminate Frenchman. But after the Gordon Riots and during the 1780s, though the old image persisted, it was accompanied by the emergence of a much tamer, safer and passive patriotic figure, the bucolic John Bull. By the 1790s the independent, beer-swilling (and somewhat radical) patriot had vanished altogether, to be replaced by either the demonic Jacobin or by the corpulent, torpid victim of processes that were beyond popular comprehension.

2. POPULAR POLITICS AS SOCIAL EMULATION c. 1760–80

Before 1790 satires of the political interests of the common people drew on a well established genre of social criticism, the critique of social emulation. Novelists, playwrights and social commentators, as well as engravers and cartoonists, lamented the growing enthusiasm of the humble for aping the fashions and the manners of the rich. As the *British Magazine* of 1763 complained, 'the present rage of imitating high life hath spread itself so far among the gentlefolks of low life, that in a few years we shall probably have no common people at all'.[21] Condemnation for demotic interest was therefore one aspect of a general disparagement of the humble's desire to exceed their station. Such presumption, it was argued, had consequences that were usually comic, sometimes tragic, and invariably unseemly. At best such forwardness in a man (or woman, for social emulation, as Dorothy George points out, was frequently equated with female social climbing)[22] would appear laughable and foolish; at worst such pretensions could lead to a person's ruin.

A Taylor Riding to Brentford (54) illustrates the price that the social and political upstart has to pay for his impertinence. A tailor, whose radical sympathies are clearly indicated by the favour marked 'Wilkes and Liberty' that he wears in his hat, is precariously mounted on a hired horse en route to the Middlesex hustings in the township of Brentford. His unsteadiness hints at a forthcoming tumble: a riding manual for beginners, 'Rules for Bad Horsemen', obtrudes from his pocket, as he desperately grips both the saddle and the horse's mane to avoid a fall. His expensive whip or cane has already reached the ground, an intimation of the fate that awaits him and his lack of control of the situation is indicated by the way he has relinquished the horse's reins. This comic scene is enjoyed by two stable lads on the left and two sweeps on the right. Exceeding one's station, we are being told, whether by interfering in politics or by hiring a horse rather than walking, is both foolish and hazardous. Pride and presumption lead to a fall.

More specifically an interest in politics was seen as an undesirable diversion or distraction which led men to neglect their proper calling. Arthur Murphy's play, *The Upholsterer*, first performed in 1758, was probably the most widely known statement of this view. His upholsterer, depicted in *43*, is a political obsessive: aided by his friend, a rumour-mongering barber who shaves ministers of state, he neglects his business, his wife and his daughter in a madcap scramble for the latest political news. Every paper, gazette and pamphlet is avidly scrutinised, every preposterous piece of hearsay treated like an eternal verity until it is superseded by another tale of more recent vintage. Not even bankruptcy can cure the upholsterer's political distemper. Time and again in the 1760s and 1770s cartoonists remind us that politics was not only divisive but led to negligence and misfortune. The title to *11* tells it all: *The Blacksmith lets his Iron grow cold attending to the Taylor's News*. The blacksmith's shop, decorated with a print of John Wilkes, has been transformed from a scene of productive industry into a venue of ill-informed and idle gossip. Popular politics, in other words, encourage sloth and depravity. As the motto on *A Meeting of City Politicians* (55) emphasises: 'With staring eye, and open Ear/Each cobling Horned City Seer/Swallows down Politics with Beer/ Neglects his Family and Calling/To enter into Party Brawling./Gets Drunk and Swears – the Nation's falling.'

3. POPULAR POLITICS AND THE MIXING OF CLASSES, 1780–90

Social and political prints, though numerous in the 1760s and 1770s – 1,033 and 964 were published in each decade – burgeoned in the 1780s: no fewer than 2,027 are listed in the British Museum Catalogue for the decade; 1784, the *annus mirabilis*, produced 410. Plebeian politics, a subject more popular than ever, was drawn in a new light: the objection to demotic politicking was no longer to its emulative and divisive character, but to the way in which it brought *together* both rich and poor. This shift cannot simply be explained by increased political fraternisation between patricians and plebs. The elder Pitt in the 1750s and John Wilkes in the 1760s and 1770s had directed their political appeal beyond the charmed circle in Westminster and both had enjoyed a warm reception. But neither of them were attacked in cartoons and caricatures for kow-towing to the common people, although this criticism was regularly levelled in pamphlets and newspapers. Yet in the 1780s, Charles James Fox, who was less radical than Wilkes, was repeatedly excoriated in the prints for breaking down the division between rich and poor, for encouraging popular political initiative, and for rubbing shoulders with the great unwashed. Before 1790 neither Pitt nor Wilkes – nor any other politician for that matter – was ever satirised *as a pleb*,[23] but Fox was depicted as a beggar (56–7), a self-seeking knifegrinder (58), a murderous butcher (59), a pugilist (60), a blacksmith (61) and, in the decade of the French revolution, as a ragged Jacobin assassin of both the monarch and the House of Commons (2, 62).

The explanation of this change is complex. Fox's conduct differed from that of Pitt and Wilkes in several important respects. Unlike his two predecessors, he was a leader of aristocratic fashion. As a youth, he had dressed as a 'macaroni', appearing in red high-heeled shoes and with blue powdered hair. He was one of the chief instigators of the fashion for 'dressing down' that began during the American war. Fox replaced the foppish and effete frippery of his youth with the blue coat and buff breeches that expressed solidarity with the American rebels: his sartorial precision gave way to a studied neglect of his appearance. Political historians forget that Fox earned the appellation, 'Man of the People', not simply because of his politics but also because of his demotic style. He and his friends were more responsible than any other group for the demise of elaborate, courtly dressing. In the words of one Georgian memoir writer,

Mr. Fox and his friends, who might be said to dictate to the town, affecting a style of neglect about their persons and manifesting a contempt of all usages hitherto established, first threw a sort of discredit on dress. From the House of Commons and the clubs of St. James's Street, the contagion spread through the private assemblies of London.[24]

Fox himself recognised the social consequences of this change in fashion. 'I have heard Fox say', wrote Lord Glenbervie, 'the neglect of dress in people of fashion had he thought contributed much to remove the barriers between them and the vulgar and profligate, levelling and equalising.'[25]

As his contemporaries recognised, Fox's conduct and attitudes were unprecedented. The elder Pitt had always held himself aloof, even from his parliamentary colleagues, and Wilkes, though he had always been prepared to eat his way through 'an ordinary' in the company of the London citizenry, was too much of a 'cit' himself to excite moral outrage by mingling with his inferiors. But Fox, who ironically began his parliamentary career with a scathing attack on the scum of London, both refashioned aristocratic style in a more plebeian mould, and created a political style that required the *beau monde* to mix with boors and blackguards.

Thus the single, corpulent figure of Charles James Fox embodied two of the chief preoccupations of the visual satirist: the vagaries of aristocratic accoutrement, which had been the staple subject matter of the Darlys' social caricatures of the 1760s and 1770s, and the response to demotic politics that we can first see in the prints of the same decades. It was now possible to predict a man's political beliefs by the style of his dress and the length of his hair. Admittedly earlier in the eighteenth century some country gentlemen had deliberately dressed in outdated styles to express their contempt for the court and their admiration for the bucolic life, but never before had the political and the sartorial been so closely and so frequently linked. When the artist Joseph Farington attended a meeting of Westminster electors in November 1795, he saw the connection as obvious. Unnerved by the radical crowd, he turned for solace to three friends, 'telling them as they were Crops (Hair cut short) and Democrats, I should be safe under their Protection'. This same gathering was hectored by the Duke of Bedford 'dressed in a Blue Coat & Buff waistcoat, with a round Hat. His Hair cropped and without powder' (cf. 63, Gillray's *Elegance Democratique*' of Lord Wycombe), and by Fox, whom Farington tersely describes as 'also cropped, and without powder, His Hair grisly grey'.[26]

This conflation of dress and politics was manna from heaven for the printmaker who was able to combine social satire and political caricature. In particular engravers were able to use the conventions of body language, dress and posture to ridicule those politicians who courted a demotic constituency. Fox is not only dressed as a despicable pleb, he has the same awkwardness and angularity (see especially 64, 65), the same lack of social grace, and the same coarse facial features (66). The opponents of Fox used all of the well established conventions to accomplish his denigration. Fox, in other words, was the victim of visual proletarianisation.

The slumming aristocrat was not only condemned for dressing down, but for his political fraternisation with the plebs. If Fox and his cronies personified this willingness to solicit the support of the humble, the highly contentious Westminster elections of the 1780s provided the stage on which this drama was acted out. The Westminster election of 1784, the most violent political contest of the Georgian era, rehearsed the chief political and social themes of the decade: the vituperative political conflict between the Foxite Whigs and their opponents led by the younger Pitt; the clash of styles between the raffish, devil-may-care antics of Carleton House and the altogether more sober and stolid conduct of George III's court; and the mingling of patrician and plebeian, a mingling that entailed close physical proximity, even intimacy, in the desperate pursuit of electoral success.

From the cartoonist's point of view the cast of characters was ideal. The dramatis personae included not only old Bluebeard – Fox himself – but the Prince of Wales, the renegade Foxite Sir Cecil Wray, the hook-nosed Admiral Hood, and a bevy of aristocratic women, most notably Mrs. Crewe, Lady Duncannon, and the ravishing Duchess of Devonshire. The visual variety of this spectacle was enhanced by the presence, for the first time in the history of the English political cartoon, of plebeians who were recognisable individuals rather than stereotypical proles. Of these two men stand out, Samuel House, a London publican, and Jeffrey Dunstan, a crippled, itinerant street seller of second-hand wigs. Between them they appear in over fifty prints in the British Museum collection.

Dunstan and House achieved notoriety because of their connection with the mock election at Garrat, a saturnalian burlesque of the electoral process that was held in a small village near Wandsworth whenever a national election was polled.[27] In the early eighteenth century this festival had been a plebeian event, an occasion of catharsis and licence at which beggars and cripples had vied for the exalted office of mock Mayor of Garrat. In the 1760s, however, the carnival drew a much larger audience. Samuel Foote made the burlesque fashionable in polite society with his extraordinarily successful comedy, the *Mayor of Garrat*, and the Wilkite radicals succeeded in politicising it during the agitation of 1768–71. Such was the mock election's popularity that the Garrat poll in 1781 was attended by a crowd of 50,000 which included members of high society as well as of low life. Coverage of the event was national: reports of the antics south of the Thames appeared in both London and provincial papers. Both Foote and the radicals pointed out that the mock election was a metaphor for the state of politics, a piece of political theatre that mimicked and mocked the grand spectacle of aristocratic political life. In the second half of the century this became a frequent and well-orchestrated theme: the Garrat election and its mock Mayor provided both visual and verbal satirists with a rich, allusive vocabulary – comparable to that derived from John Gay's *Beggar's Opera* earlier in the century – with which to lampoon both patrician and plebeian politicians.

Jeffrey Dunstan, or 'Sir Jeffrey' as he was known, was an unsuccessful candidate for Garrat in 1781, when he ran on an overtly anti-government ticket, and Mayor from 1785 to 1796. Doubtless Dunstan's success as a candidate – and one of the reasons why he was taken up by the political cartoonist – was due to his grotesque appearance. Knock-kneed, hunched-up, his wig-bag tossed over his shoulder and with one hand raised as he cried his wares, Dunstan was a walking violation of the precepts of gentility, the physical embodiment of a vulgar prole. Lairesse in his painting manual could hardly have found a more suitable subject with which to personify the physical characteristics of the common man. Dunstan, in other words, was both distinctive – a suitable subject for caricature – and archetypal. His physiognomy, his inane grin and vacant stare, made him a figure of fun, an ideal means of satirising the political pretensions of the humble. Thus in *The Robin Hood Society* (67), Dunstan, in his usual pose, hand raised and wig-bag over his shoulder, addresses the debating club, whose members are grossly caricatured with imbecilic, saturnine and simian faces. On the wall in the background hangs Dunstan's portrait (he is wearing a civic chain and carrying a mace, clear reference to the mayoralty of Garrat), while a future motion of the society is advertised as 'How far is it from the first of Augt to the foot of Westminster Bridge'. The intent of the print is clear: to deride popular ambitions and portray popular political concerns as arrant nonsense.

This uncharitable picture of Dunstan and of popular politics derives much of its force from its association with the Garrat election as a burlesque and with the Mayor of Garrat as 'the fool of the fair'. But there was another side to the mock election and to Sir Jeffrey Dunstan. The Wilkite radicals of the 1760s had used the election as a didactic spectacle, as means of disseminating their critique of the government, the court, and of political corruption. From the radical point of view the plebeian candidates were not therefore subject to mockery because they were plebeian; rather spectators laughed at their representation of *patrician* vices and follies. The festival had the purpose 'of producing those reforms by means of ridicule and shame, which are vainly expected from solemn appeals of argument and patriotism'.[28] This overt politicisation of the mock election attracted some humble men to Garrat because of the opportunity it afforded them to make their political sentiments publicly known. The character of both the speeches and the candidates changed: controversial political issues were explicitly addressed, and those who stood for election were now drawn not just from the hamlet of Garrat but from the entire metropolitan area.

Jeffrey Dunstan was such a candidate. No doubt his grotesque appearance and reputation as a prodigious drinker help explain his presence at Garrat, but he was also a man of strongly held radical opinions. In his platform speech of 1781 he attacked Lord North, supported the American colonists, criticised the recent increase in excise taxes on beer, and condemned forestallers who artificially raised the prices of basic commodities. During the repression of the 1790s he was imprisoned for his radical views.

Equally Sam House, though described by his contemporaries as an 'ODDITY', had serious political pretensions. House was a flamboyant Wardour Street publican who combined radical politics, great industry and a singular ability for self-advertisement. Though never voted Mayor of Garrat, he seems to have stood unsuccessfully for election in 1781 and he was certainly closely associated with a number of the other candidates, who would meet to drink together at his hostelry (68). House first achieved notoriety in the 1760s by jumping off Westminster Bridge for a wager: 'the singular feat of activity, by everyone thought impossible, without occasioning immediate death, rendered him a popular character, and filled his house with customers'. During the same decade House first became involved in radical politics as a supporter of John Wilkes. His political creed is aptly summarised by his declaration at the Westminster Poll of 1784. When asked to state his employment he replied, 'Sir, I am a publican and a republican.'[29]

House's appearance was extraordinary. Rowlandson's drawing and print of 1780 (69, 70) captured his cheerful pugnacity. He was totally bald with the heavyset bulldog features of a prize fighter. House never varied his dress: he always wore a long, dark waistcoat, refusing the formality of either a wig or a coat. His shirts, reputedly made of the best linen, were left open at the neck, his breeches were not fastened at the knee. His occasional head-dress consisted of a large floppy-brimmed hat. His sartorial taste, which endeared him to the visual satirist, was described as 'not only singular, but laughably ridiculous'. Yet, as Rowlandson shows, House was not a man to be trifled with. His portrayal of House, legs apart and planted firmly on the ground (a stance that is neither aristocratic nor demotic, though it is certainly assertive), belly thrust forward, a brimming tankard in his hand, conveys both the self-esteem of a man who saw himself as 'a true-born Englishman', and the robust integrity of a liberty-loving patriot. As his obituary remarked, 'he was never embarrassed in the presence of any man, and though he frequently called upon the great, he never changed his dress or his character'.[30]

The distinctive and radically different features of Dunstan and House made it possible for the political cartoonist to produce genuine caricatures of aspiring humble politicians. Before the 1780s plebeian politicians were either anonymous faces in the crowd or they were identified, as we have seen, by the costume of their trade or calling. This has led one eighteenth-century historian to remark that, 'to speak of the caricature of the eighteenth-century mob is, in a sense, a contradiction in terms. Caricature, as a graphic technique, pertains to individuals and not to the impersonal mass.'[31] But thanks to the notoriety of the Garrat election and its flamboyant participants, it became possible to distinguish plebeian as well as patrician faces in the crowd: House and Dunstan were as readily recognised (and caricatured) as the more genteel figures of Fox, Pitt and Burke.

Thus in the humble audience that Fox harangues in an anti-Foxite cartoon of 1783 (23), Dunstan, clearly distinguishable from the rest of the mob, stands in the foreground, declaring, 'Thank Heaven the people have such a friend'. House is found in similar postures. In different cartoons – two favourable and one hostile – of Fox's triumphal procession after his return at the Westminster election of 1784, House is placed in a prominent position in the crowd: huzzahing Fox and waving his wide-brimmed, floppy hat (71) – a pose that Rowlandson uses in his depiction of House in his *Procession to the Hustings after a Successful Canvass* (72) – actually helping bear Fox in his chair (73), or leading a dangerous and unprepossessing group of cleaver-carrying butchers marching under a banner marked 'Marrow Bones and Cleavers Constitutional Supporters' (74).

House's presence in these Foxite parades and demonstrations is only partly attributable to his association with the Garrat election. Of greater significance was his role as a political organiser for Fox in the actual Westminster elections of 1780 and 1784. Indeed, together with the Duchess of Devonshire, House was the single most conspicuous figure working for Fox in 1784. House's role is aptly captured in Rowlandson's print, *The Westminster Deserter Drum'd out of the Regiment* (75): he was the drum-major who called to arms the serried ranks of Foxites. No-one contributed more to the mobilisation of the poorer constituents of Westminster: they marched to his beat.

As archetypal plebeian politician and as one of Fox's campaign managers (the term is not anachronistic in this context), House became the focus of much of the comment, both in the press and in prints, on the co-mingling of the classes. He was used by cartoonists either to represent the demotic following of Fox or as a link between the high society of Carlton House and the low life of Westminster's lanes and alleys. In *Mr*

Fox addressing his Friends from the King's Arms Tavern Feb 14, 1784 (76), House can be seen in an adulatory crowd that hangs on to Fox's every word: the second figure on his left is Dunstan, recognisable by his wig-bag and knock-kneed stance. The crowd also includes a lamp-lighter, a carter, a sweep, a butcher and a rat-catcher. The implications of this print are clearly anti-Foxite; the proletarian character of Fox's audience both condemns him for appealing to such a disreputable group and also implies that such riff-raff are the only sort of following that he is able to command (cf. 77).

Though much of the criticism of Fox's political tactics and of the type of politics they engendered was effected through his association with Sam House, it was the connection between the Wardour Street publican and the Duchess of Devonshire that particularly attracted political cartoonists. Georgina and Sam had much in common: a passionate adherence to the Foxite cause, close personal friendship with Fox himself, and a seemingly indefatigable enthusiasm for electoral canvassing. Above all they each represented the aristocratic and plebeian facets of the new politics: the Duchess's willingness to canvass butchers, chimney-sweeps and cobblers (78) showed that the rules of the political game had been changed, while House's refusal to defer to his social superiors was symptomatic of a novel political assertiveness amongst the humble.

House and the Duchess were portrayed supping together from tankards of ale (79), canvassing together (78), marching in parades side by side (72), and dancing hand in hand (80). It was rumoured that they planned to elope and that 'If Karlo Khan (ie. Fox) succeeds at Westminster, *Lord Derby* is to give another fete champetre, and *Sam House* and *her Grace* are to open the ball with a minuet in a new style; they have already received lessons.' (A similar rumour was circulated about Jeffrey Dunstan and the Duchess of Portland.)[32]

For all that they held in common, House and the Duchess caught the cartoonist's eye because of the marvellous visual contrast that they presented. The two were repeatedly juxtaposed to reveal the socially anomalous situation bred by Foxite politics and the antics of the Westminster election. House, plebeian, virile, ugly and coarse-featured was contrasted with the Duchess, a stunning aristocratic beauty, whose delicate frame, decked out in the latest fashion, represented in exquisite form the most refined and genteel elements of polite society. House and the Duchess presented complementary though contrasting images: they face one another as they clank their tankards together (79), or occupy mirror positions at either end of the hustings in Covent Garden (81). Their union is presented as both intimate and incongruous: at best a rib-tickling joke and at worst an unnatural relationship in the worst of taste. Rowlandson brilliantly captured the shocking nature of this familiarity in his *Lords of the Bedchamber* (82). Instead of portraying the Duchess, House and Fox out on the street 'pressing flesh' and winning votes (as he had in *Wit's Last Stake* (78)), he places them in the intimate surroundings of the Duchess's boudoir. This domestic setting – the Duchess is décolletée – makes their camaraderie all the more outrageous. It was bad enough that the plebeian House should rub shoulders with the Duchess in public, but it was truly horrifying to find him sharing her morning cup of tea in the privacy of her own closet.

There is a strong sexual undertone to the depictions of House and the Duchess. *The Election Tete à Tete* (*79*) is as much a print of a lad and his moll out on the town, drinking in Covent Garden – the location of London's finest bordellos and bagnios – as it is about the meeting of two of Fox's political allies. House, whose posthumous biography contains several anecdotes that leave us with very little doubt of his sexual prowess, was clearly a man with a large, uninhibited sensual appetite. He personifies the straightforward, direct sexuality of the plebeian who is unrestrained by genteel convention. The Duchess, who lived in a notorious *ménage à trois* and who had many much publicised affairs, is both condemned in the prints as an aristocratic tramp and used to imply that aristocratic men have become so effete and effeminate that only stout-hearted plebs can satisfy her desires. In print after print Georgina is depicted in the arms of stalwart butchers. Sexual innuendo abounds: the Duchess canvasses for 'her favourite member' in Cockspur Street (*83*), she dances with a butcher whose apron is inscribed 'All upright Members for ever' (*84*), and in three of the prints (*85–7*), a cleaver is prominently displayed in a deliberate reference to the slang 'a cleaver', meaning, 'a wanton woman; one that will cleave'.[33] The Duchess was understandably infuriated by this portrayal of her as a lascivious trollop. House deliberately avoided her during the canvass in a futile attempt to stop the spread of more mendacious stories of her lubricious conduct. But many applauded the prints. As one paper reported:

The print-shops exhibit in the most striking colours the depravity of the present day, and laudably expose the temporary familiarity *so very predominant between the great and the little vulgar. When titled persons deign to become associates with the lowest publicans [a clear reference to House], to copy their manner, and meanly solicit their favours, the sarcasms and indecencies to which they expose themselves cannot be too plainly and too publicly held out as the just rewards of an affected humility and specious condescension.*[34]

The Duchess and her stout butchers, House and his aristocratic cronies, Fox in a coat with no elbows: each of these scenes reminds us of 'the *temporary familiarity* so very predominant between the great and the little vulgar' which was one of the dominant themes of visual satire in the 1780s. During these years it is impossible to distinguish, as it was both earlier and later, the portrayal of the common people in politics from the depiction of political activity as a whole. On the rare occasions that a pleb was shown without aristocratic company the patrician presence is still felt. Thus in Rowlandson's wonderful print of Sam House (*70*) we are reminded of his association with Fox by the inscription on the large beer-barrel that House's massive torso partly conceals (cf. the punchbowl in *88*).

The politics of the 1780s, as it appeared in the print shops, was a matter of antinomies. The rotund, bushy-eyebrowed Fox faces the austere stick-like Pitt; the profligate youth of Carlton House opposed the middle-aged, uxorious respectability of

George III; and the great unwashed – a city of street sellers, butchers and publicans – debated with peers and parliamentary politicians. The depiction of this last development was both complex and ambivalent. There are no prints that overtly approve the mixing of gentleman with commoner, though some of the Foxite characters (e.g. *71*) are clearly sympathetic. One the other hand, none of the cartoons of the common people was etched in vitriol: they never exhibit the almost pathological fear and loathing, the revulsion that can be found in the anti-radical prints after the outbreak of the French Revolution. The dialogue between the genteel and the plebeian politician has not broken down; indeed, it is very much alive and the chief focus of attention. Rich and poor are portrayed as speaking the same political language and sharing many political assumptions. Sam House may defer to no man and Fox may need his political friendship, but House works for Fox, he does not organise his own political movement or intrigue to reform or subvert the constitution. He may demand that every patriotic Englishman have a say in politics, but, apart from the issue of participation, House's politics is very much politics as usual: he is an old style Patriot, a 'Liberty Boy', rather than a new style reformer.

Although many, perhaps most, of the prints poke fun at the political pretensions of Sam House and Jeffrey Dunstan, they also accord the plebeian politicians a begrudging respect, even admiration. The pugnacious, earthy self-regard shown by the common people, their determination to protect their rights and liberties, appear to be seen as the necessary price to be paid for a free constitution. In this sense, House and Dunstan enjoy a certain licence, they enter the political arena with the (somewhat begrudging) approval of their superiors. Though no doubt House and Dunstan would have vigorously denied it, they were tame, domesticated and therefore unthreatening popular politicians. Certainly Rowlandson knew this: even as *Lords of the Bedchamber* (*82*) shocks us by showing Sam House in the Duchess's boudoir, it reassures us by showing Fox patting House benignly on the head. The begging lap-dog at the Duchess's feet mirrors House's pug-like posture: he is the aristocrats' pet pleb (cf. *89* where House is the Duchess's link-boy).

Sam House, in other words, caused more amusement than trepidation amongst the propertied classes. As we have seen, this was the typical response in the prints to most plebeian political initiative during the 1780s. One set of incidents, however, provoked the fright and horror which we more usually associate with the reaction to the coming of the French Revolution. They also engendered the first cartoons to portray a more sinister and malevolent popular politician – the destroyer of property and the desecrator of the nation's hallowed institutions (*44, 90*). The zealous activities of the Protestant Association, a body implacably opposed to conferring on Catholics the same civil rights as those enjoyed by patriotic protestants, and the tumultuous Gordon Riots which followed the presentation to Parliament of the Association's monster petition against Catholic Relief, struck fear into the hearts of many propertied Englishmen. The six days of rioting – from 2 to 8 June 1780 – were the worst in the history of eighteenth-century London. £70,000 worth of damage was done to private property –

Catholic premises and the houses of such aristocratic sympathisers as Lord Mansfield – 285 men and women died, chiefly at the hands of the military, Newgate gaol was stormed and ransacked (thereby providing the most popular subject for the prints of the riot – see 51–3), prisoners were freed from the King's Bench prison, the New Gaol and the Marshalsea, and the Bank of England was unsuccessfully attacked. Ten thousand troops had to be used to restore order.

Such mayhem provoked a far stronger reaction than the benign condescension conferred on Sam House (though House was a supporter of the Protestant Association). The prints of *A Petitioning, Remonstrating, Reforming, Republican* (44) and of *No Popery or Newgate Reformer* (90) both lack the good humour and playfulness that is characteristic of so many of the Westminster election prints that depict House and Dunstan. 'The Republican' defiles both church and state, using a mitre for a piss-pot and a crown for his privy, while the so-called 'Newgate Reformer' proves to be a thinly-disguised blackguard or footpad, bent only on rapine and plunder. These opprobrious prints prefigure the savage satires of radical popular politics that filled the print-shop windows in the 1790s. Their acerbity, however, does not match the asperity of the anti-Jacobin cartoons of the French Revolutionary era. Both 'the Republican' and the 'Newgate Reformer', though far from strong contenders in a beauty contest, bear a passing resemblance to familiar human figures. They are neither as simian nor as grotesque as, to take one fairly typical example of Gillray's work, the members of the radical London Corresponding Society depicted in 91. In the prints of the 1780s the plebeian politician is still a member of the species *Homo sapiens*; he may be reprehensible but he still belongs within the realms of ordinary experience. But Gillray's figures, despite his use of the metonymic conventions to identify the butcher and the barber, do not belong to this earth: with the exception of the pipe-smoking butcher who resembles Gale Jones, the radical surgeon, they are all preternatural, monstrous creatures, skulking in the stygian gloom. Here is a picture of hell and its inhabitants – the tankard on the table is inscribed 'Tom Treason *Hell-Fire* Cellar, Chick Lane'.

4. POPULAR POLITICS AND SATANIC RADICALS, THE 1790s

In Gillray's work, as in most prints of the 1790s, plebeian politicians, especially those who embraced the ideas of Tom Paine (whom Gillray savagely satirised as 'the little American Taylor' in *The Rights of Man* (92), forfeited all semblance of human dignity. Gillray's most ferocious attacks on French Revolutionary ideas, however, usually occur in a foreign rather than a domestic context. His scathing depiction of the Irish rebels of 1798 – *United Irishmen on Duty* and *United Irishmen in Training* (93, 94) – combines the long-standing anti-Irish chauvinism of the English with Gillray's singular antipathy towards radicals, regardless of their nationality. But even these prints are no match for his venomous anti-French work. These cartoons are both numerous and well known (eg. *95, 96*), especially the series of 1798 entitled *Consequences of a Successful French Invasion* (*61, 97, 98*). They combine an extraordinary intensity of feeling, a high degree of compression, with brilliant, vivid images. *Petit Souper, a la Parisienne* (*99*), prompted by the September massacres of 1792, epitomises the genre. Gillray depicts the hideous cannibalism of a sans culottes family. Three generations of radical Parisians gorge themselves on human vitals, guzzle down human limbs, and baste a baby over an open fire.

Though nothing so grotesque or terrifying appears in an English context, British radicals were condemned by association. In *Patriotic Regeneration* (*100*), prime minister William Pitt is impeached before a parliament 'reform'd, à la Francoise', and which therefore consists of English working men. The same occupational stereotypes – the butcher, the sweep, the tailor, the hairdresser – that had appeared in prints throughout the century are seen on the benches of the House of Commons. But the figures differ from their precursors: they are grosser, more distorted, exhibiting a new ferocity, malice and brutishness. The noxious distemper of French democratic ideas has infected the humble, free-born Englishman, sapping his strength and tainting his virtue; all that remains is the demoralised brute, a degenerate creature, French in all but name.

The contrast with even the most pejorative depictions of humble politicians before the 1790s is an obvious one. The earlier figures (eg. *12* etc.) conform to the precepts of Lairesse: they are awkward and angular, they have comic, foolish and uncomprehending faces, they lack the elegance and poise of their social superiors. Their appearance indicates both their social status and their moral worth: neither are particularly high. On the other hand, the figures are neither malevolent, inhuman or terrifying. They inspire amusement, pathos and a little magnanimity: the rich, the propertied and the financially secure can afford both to laugh and be kind to these pathetic figures because they do not threaten them: the activities of demotic politicians do not provoke strong passions. But before 1790 it did not seem likely that the last aristocrat would be strangled with the guts of the last priest; by 1792 this seemed more than a remote possibility. The emotion provoked among the English aristocracy as well as the doyens of Versailles was of terror and awe: the highest and most powerful sensation of the 'sublime'. Ronald Paulson has recently pointed out that much of the imagery of the Revolution's most implacable opponent, Edmund Burke, is derived from 'the terrible of the sublime'.[35] A similar case could, I think, be made for Gillray and some of his fellow cartoonists. The aesthetics of Lairesse provided a visual language whose limited vocabulary could only chide or issue a mild and condescending rebuke. More powerful stuff was needed to curb revolutionary distemper. It was no longer sufficient to see the plebeian politician as risible; the artist needed a new and more powerful means of conveying the grotesque, satanic enormity of humble men's defiance of the *natural* order of things.

5. THE ARCHETYPAL ENGLISHMAN:
JOHN BULL AND HIS PREDECESSORS 1730–1800

This escalating antipathy towards all popular politicians has a parallel history in the changing stereotype of the archetypal Englishman. The 1790s were indubitably the decade of John Bull: the number of prints of the bovine Briton far outnumbered all previous depictions of him. And, as Draper Hill remarks, Bull 'rarely performs in an aggressive capacity. Devotedly patriotic, he exists primarily as an object for harassment and exploitation.'[36] But, just as demotic politicians had not always been depicted as grimacing baboons, so the patriotic pleb had not always appeared so tractable and docile. Indeed, although there were relatively few portrayals of representative patriotic Englishmen before 1790 and even fewer that were explicitly named John Bull, those that did appear invariably depicted a far more indomitable and stout-hearted Brition than the pusillanimous and bemused figure to be found in the prints of the century's final decade. Sailors and butchers – men never thought of as timorous or faint-hearted – most frequently represented their fellow citizens: they were contrasted either with foreigners or with effeminate fops.

The choice of sailors as archetypal Englishmen is easy to understand. England's navies – merchant and royal – were a source of national pride both as the life-line of the nation's commerce, the carrier of its imperial wealth, and as the chief bulwark of the nation's defence. Sailors – humble merchant seamen and jack tars as well as Admirals like Vernon, Rodney, Hood and Nelson – enjoyed a special place in that concatenation of symbols and values that were thought of as distinctively English.

The heroic stature accorded the English sailor can be seen in *The British Hercules* (8), where a humble tar is portrayed in the manner of the Farnese Hercules. The neo-classical portrayal imparts a dignity and strength that is rarely seen in depictions of the common people, and which directly defies the aesthetic principles laid down by such academicians as Lairesse. The print of 1737 criticised a supine administration which was reluctant to mobilise the navy against the Spanish. But the Herculean sailor who rests from his prodigious labours seems to represent more than his fellow tars: he stands for a powerful nation and a strong people, who are eager to enter the fray, but who are held in check by a peace-loving and chicken-hearted Whig government. This same nautical belligerence can be seen in *The St-te Quack (101)*, one of the many attacks on Lord Bute and his Scottish compatriots that appeared in the 1760s. An irate sailor, clearly representative of the English, thrashes a skinny, kilted Scot while bitterly complaining of Lord Bute's political malpractice.

The patriotic butcher, though a less obvious candidate for the part of the representative, liberty-loving Englishman, shared many of the qualities of his seaman colleague. His work required skill, strength and a lack of squeamishness; he was typically thought of in the eighteenth century as both bold and, like the sailor on shore, extremely amorous. (The latter characteristic of butchers was successfully exploited in the prints of the 1784 Westminster election.) And if sailors protected the nation, butchers presided over the preparation and sale of that most distinctive of English dishes, the roast beef of England.

The prints linked national identity to culinary and dietary habits. The Englishman's dinner-table groaned under the weight of huge cuts of roast beef, brimming tankards of good English ale, and vast puddings, the very sight of which would induce dyspepsia (*102, 103*). These magnificent meals were the cartoonists' symbol of good fortune and prosperity enjoyed, it was maintained, by every freeborn Englishman. Such gastronomic plenitude was contrasted with the meagre diet and exotic victuals of the French. Foul-tasting garlic, snails and the miserable frog were the exiguous Gallic staple (*102, 103*). Such was the poverty of the French nation and the culinary perversity of its people. The English butcher, therefore, was not only the personification of English virility but a reminder of English prosperity.

The guardians of the nation's finest dish would endure no slight or insult: they personified the citizen who in Edward Thompson's words, knows 'the *limits* beyond which the Englishman was not prepared to be 'pushed around".[37] The point is well made in an amusing print of 1747, *The Beaux Disaster* (*104*). A fussy aristocratic fop pays a high price for his haughty and overbearing conduct towards butchers on the Strand: 'But they unus'd Affront to brook,/Have hung poor Fribble on a Hook.' The contrast here is between aristocratic prissiness and effeminacy (qualities to be found in David Garrick's Fribble in *Miss in her Teens*) and the masculine, unaffected directness of the demotic butcher. This same theme was given a chauvinist twist in the 1770s. Two prints, *The Frenchman at Market* (*105*), and the mezzotint, *The Frenchman in London* with its motto, 'Foreign Gentlemen taught English' (*106*), both portray an altercation between a stocky English butcher and a thin, effete Frenchman. The Frenchman has apparently complained that the dirty, greasy butcher has rubbed up against him. Such foreign hauteur is shortly to be rewarded with a hearty English drubbing. Both prints treat French gent and English butcher as visual and moral antitheses: the former is a mincing coward, the latter, even when portrayed as considerably smaller than his opponent, is proud, fearless and resolute. If we glance again at Rowlandson's portrayal of Sam House (*69, 70*), we can see how House's stocky, stalwart figure fits into this tradition of patriotic pugnacity.

Not all of the prints of true-born Englishmen fit this pre-French Revolutionary pattern of combative chauvinism. Indeed the first explicit portrayal of John Bull (*107*), a powerful and highly effective depiction of the Scottish burden borne by the English nation in the 1760s, prefigures the prints of the 1790s in showing Bull as a wretched and uncomprehending victim. But *A Poor Man Loaded with Mischief* is very much the exception that proves the rule. Before the 1790s, the true Englishman, whether a cook (*108*) or a farmer (*109*), is a robust and proud character whose moral and physical strength is sustained by overflowing tankards of ale and large loins of beef.

The contrast after 1790 could hardly be more marked. Admittedly there were a few prints – most notably '*Treason!!*' (*110*) – which show Bull as the irreverent Briton who is no respecter of persons. Equally there was the occasional depiction of a confrontation between Bull and the French in which the former triumphed (*111*). But even in these prints Bull has lost his dignity. He is either a broad-grinning buffoon (as in *110*), a dim-witted, grossly overweight glutton (*102*), or the child-like simpleton – a gross caricature of the rustic fool (*112, 113*) – incapable of altering his fate either as the dupe of French radicals (*114*), as cannon-fodder in a protracted war (*115*), or as the victim of repressive domestic legislation (*116–19*).

CONCLUSION

At the end of the century, therefore, the political cartoonist took as hostile or as opprobrious a view of the plebeian as he did at any point in the eighteenth century. The old, liberty-loving robust figure that antedated the French Revolution had been torn asunder by a process of visual schizophrenia, divided into two personalities, the wicked radical and the half-wit patriot.

Some historians have suggested that the political cartoon played an important role in democratising politics in the late eighteenth century. The content of cartoons, it is pointed out, was less exclusively aristocratic and the market for prints more widely ramified. Several sacred cows – most notably the monarch himself – were no longer treated reverentially, yet engravers increasingly autographed their work, apparently indicating that they had ceased to fear government prosecution.[38]

Our discussion of the common people forcibly indicates the limitations of this view. Plebeians may have featured more frequently in cartoons towards the end of the century, but throughout the period popular politics was portrayed as an unseemly aberration. Legitimate politics was a matter of aristocratic and genteel leadership, of orderliness and of a hierarchy in which every man and woman knew their place. Radical politicians could draw little consolation or comfort from the great majority of political satires. The assumptions of cartoonists and engravers about popular politics were both constant and conservative – only the treatment of this undesirable phenomenon changed. When plebeian politics seemed more risible than menacing, the prints used a combination of satire and witty disparagement; when the common people constituted a genuine threat, they were overtly and viciously attacked, execrated as radicals, jeered at as buffoons.

Why does the radicalism of the 1790s seem to have excited so little sympathy in the political prints? It is possible of course, that the British Museum collection of personal and political satires does not present a complete picture of radical engraving. The provenance of the collection is genteel and it contains very few woodcuts or crude examples of engraving, some of which prefigure the world of William Hone in their sympathetic attitude towards popular politics. Equally the radical hermeneutics of William Blake are poorly represented; we seem to be a far cry from the apocalyptic world of radical engravers and printers so brilliantly depicted by David Erdman.[39]

We must remember, however, the constraints that existed on the print trade. The structure and character of the industry was such that most prints were undoubtedly intended for an audience that was aristocratic, genteel and often bourgeois. By the 1790s print production and distribution was a sophisticated business with a considerable division of labour. The artist who produced the original drawing, the engraver who prepared the copper-plate, the shopmen who pressed and dried the print, the women

45

and children who coloured the final product: all of these different individuals were to varying degrees dependent upon the linch-pin of the print trade, the printseller. It was he (or often she) who published and marketed the product (and therefore had legal responsiblity for its content) and who, in the final analysis, determined what was sold to the public. By the end of the century the print trade was dominated by a few powerful and prosperous printsellers. They were not about to jeopardise their stable position and control of the market by a rash flirtation with political views that in the heady days of the French Revolution smacked of treason. They were not afraid to produce satires in the Whig oppositionist tradition that lauded Englishmen's rights and attacked the Crown: hence the prints criticising the invasion of subjects' rights in 1795 and monarchical miserliness throughout the decade. Printsellers knew that they could rely on the sympathy and possibly the protection of the genteel opponents of Pitt and George III. Natural rights radicalism was, however, both a different kettle of fish and a much bigger business risk. The printsellers, in other words, operated within the realm of financial prudence and of acceptable political discourse.

We should also not assume that prints attacking popular politics were never viewed or applauded by the humble. Though there can be little doubt that most prints *were intended* for an audience that was aristocratic, genteel and often bourgeois – and therefore embodied an appropriately proper and conservative set of values – it is equally beyond dispute that cartoons reached a larger audience. Though almost none of the labouring poor and probably few artisans and master craftsmen *bought* prints, they nevertheless would have seen them in print-shop windows, in taverns and coffee-houses, and in the homes of their social superiors.

What was the popular reaction to these prints? Did the poorer members of society see cartoons portraying the common people and politics in the same way as the more affluent men who patronised the print shops? There is almost no surviving evidence, other than the prints themselves, that enables us to answer this question. Using predominantly internal evidence, Ronald Paulson has recently argued that Hogarth's work often lends itself to more than one reading and was designed for more than one audience. *Industry and Idleness*, for example, is interpreted both as a hortatory moral tract and as a deliberate subversion of the simple equation that linked industry and virtue, idleness and vice.[40]

Can we perhaps see a similar ambiguity or double-entendre in the political prints? It would not surprise me to discover that a number of the cartoons that satirised plebeian politics before the 1790s were construed as sympathetic to the phenomenon that they playfully criticised. I have already remarked on the ambiguity with which the patriotic Englishman was treated before the French Revolution and on the begrudging respect accorded to the different tradesmen and street sellers – the Sam Houses and Jeffrey Dunstans – who flung themselves into politics. A print such as *The Politicians* (22), despite its satire of plebeian political enthusiasm, might well have been admired by the humble simply because it showed them as political agents. The admission that popular politics existed was probably sufficient cause to excite the interest and approbation of the poor. However, after 1790 and before the overtly radical prints of the early nineteenth century, the political message of the prints was altogether less ambiguous. Nevertheless there may well have been loyal plebs – it would be a mistake to assume that popular politics is invariably radical or reformist – who sympathised with the plight of helpless John Bull. But how numerous such men were remains a mystery.

What can the historian learn from the many prints that portrayed the common people and politics? First and foremost, he can recover a set of socially discriminatory attitudes towards plebeian political participation. Admittedly there are other, more traditional sources from which we can derive these views, but these do not reveal, as the prints do, the visual dimension to the exercise of authority and to the expression of social superiority. The theatrical dimension to politics – a favourite theme of recent eighteenth-century historiography[41] – is enormously illuminated by an examination of the prints. Historians have reconstructed eighteenth-century political rhetoric – the character and conventions that circumscribed political debate – but they have yet to reconstitute the visual syntax of eighteenth-century political power. Cartoons are a vital source for this enterprise, for nowhere else do the politics of aesthetics and the aesthetics of politics so explicitly converge.

FOOTNOTES

1. E. H. Gombrich, 'The Cartoonist's Armoury', *Meditations on a Hobby Horse* (3rd ed., London, 1978), pp. 127–42.

2. David Alexander and Richard T. Godfrey, *Painters and Engraving, The Reproductive Print from Hogarth to Wilkie* (Yale Center for British Art, New Haven, 1980), p. 14.

3. Quoted in Ronald Paulson, *Hogarth: His Life, Art, and Times* (2 vols., London, 1971), I, p. 140.

4. Alexander and Godfrey, *Painters and Engraving*, catalogue no. 120; Cf. ibid., catalogue no. 145. See also the very important work of John Barrell on Morland: *The Dark Side of the Landscape: The Rural Poor in English Painting 1730–1840* (Cambridge, 1980), ch. 2.

5. Sir Ambrose Heal, *London Tradesmen's Cards of the XVIIIth Century, An Account of their Origin and Use* (London, 1925), passim.

6. Paulson, *Hogarth*, I, p. 167.

7. Gerard de Lairesse, *The Art of Painting in all its Branches, methodically demonstrated by Discourses and Plates, and exemplified by remarks on the paintings of the best Masters; and their perfections and oversights laid open*, trans. John Frederick Fritsch (London 1778); *Caractères des passions, sur les dessins de C. le Brun. A Drawing Book of the Passions, from the designs of C. le Brun* (London, 1750).

8. Lairesse, *The Art of Painting*, p. 31.

9. Lairesse, ibid., p. 33.

10. *The Man of Manners or the Plebeian Polished* (London, 1735).

11. F. Nivelon, *The Rudiments of Genteel Behaviour* (London, 1737), p. 6.

12. *The Man of Manners*, p. 9.

13. Lairesse, *The Art of Painting*, p. 31.

14. Alaisdair Smart, 'Dramatic Gesture and Expression in the Age of Hogarth and Reynolds', *Apollo* 82 (1965), pp. 90–7.

15. George Alexander Stevens, *A New Lecture on Heads* (London & Boston, 1772), p. 51.

16. This point is made explicitly in the appendix, 'Essay on Satire', to *A Lecture on Heads by Geo. Alex Stevens, with additions, as delivered by Mr. Charles Lee Lewes* (London, 1808), pp. 1–91 (second pagination).

17. Quoted in M. D. George, *Hogarth to Cruickshank: Social Change in Graphic Satire* (London, 1967), p. 16.

18. [Addison], *The Spectator* CCLI (18 December 1711).

19. W. Roberts, *The Cries of London* (London, 1924) passim; Robert Raines, *Marcellus Laroon* (London, 1966), pp. 15–17, 95–100.

20. Elias Canetti, *Crowds and Power* (Penguin ed., London, 1973), pp. 21–4, 32.

21. Quoted in George, *Hogarth to Cruickshank*, p. 64.

22. George, ibid., p. 64.

23. There are occasional references to politicians as plebs earlier in the century (see BMC 3021) but they never have the personal associations that we find with Fox.

24. Wraxall quoted in George, *Hogarth to Cruickshank*, p. 136.

25. George, ibid., p. 136.

26. *The Diary of Joseph Farington*, ed. Kenneth Garlick and Angus Macintyre (6 vols. to date, New Haven, 1978–), II, pp. 404–5.

27. For a fuller description of the Garrat

election see John Brewer, 'Theater and Counter-Theater in Georgian Politics: The Mock Elections at Garrat', *Radical History Review* 22 (1979–80), pp. 7–40.

28. *A Description of the Mock Election at Garrat, on the Seventh of this Month, Wherein is given some Historical Account of its first rise, and the curious Cavalcades of the Different Candidates, the speeches they made at the Hustings, the whimsical oath of Qualification, and an authentic Copy of their several droll Printed Addresses* (London, 1768).

29. *The Life and Opinions of the late Sam House; interspersed with curious anecdotes and amorous intrigues of this singular and distinguished character. Published by Authority, from Authentic Documents* (London, 1785), passim.

30. *Gentleman's Magazine* (1785), pp. 326–9.

31. Herbert M. Atherton, 'The Mob in Eighteenth-Century Caricature', *Eighteenth-Century Studies* 12, 1 (1978), p. 47.

32. *A History of the Westminster Election, containing every material occurrence, from its commencement on the first of April, to the final close of the poll, on the 17th of May* (London, 1784), pp. 94, 228, 270, 327.

33. *1811 Dictionary of the Vulgar Tongue* (repr., Northfield, Ill., 1971), no pagination.

34. *History of the Westminster Election*, p. 253.

35. Ronald Paulson, 'Burke's Sublime and the Representation of Revolution', *Culture and Politics from Puritanism to the Enlightenment*, ed. Perez Zagorin (London, 1980), p. 250.

36. Draper Hill, *Mr. Gillray, Caricaturist* (London, 1965), p. 46, but contrast M. D. George's remarks (M. D. George, *English Political Caricature, vol. 1, to 1792* (Oxford, 1959), p. 177).

37. E. P. Thompson, *The Making of the English Working Class* (London, 1965), p. 87.

38. Charles Press, 'The Georgian Political Print and Democratic Institutions', *Comparative Studies in Society and History* 19 no. 2 (1977), pp. 216–38.

39. David Erdman, *Blake, Prophet Against Empire* (Princeton, 1954), passim.

40. Ronald Paulson, *Emblem and Expression: Meaning in English Art of the Eighteenth Century* (Cambridge, Mass., 1975), ch. 5.

41. Edward Thompson, 'Patrician Society, Plebeian Culture', *Journal of Social History* 7 (1974), esp. pp. 389–90, 396, 402; Edward Thompson, 'Eighteenth-Century English Society: Class Struggle without Class?', *Social History* 3 (1978), esp. pp. 145–6; Douglas Hay, 'Property, Authority and the Criminal Law', *Albion's Fatal Tree*, ed. Douglas Hay, Peter Linebaugh, E. P. Thompson (London, 1975), pp. 25–31.

THE PLATES

These notes are prefixed with the relevant number in the *Catalogue of Political and Personal Satires Preserved in the Department of Prints and Drawings in the British Museum* (eds. F. G. Stephens and M. D. George) 11 vols. 1870–1954, which should be consulted for further information. This is followed by the date of publication and engraver, where known.

1. BMC 4033   April 1763
   The Scotch Yoke; or English Resentment
   A typical attack on the Scotch royal favourite, Lord Bute, especially directed at
   the excise tax on cider of 1763. Note the different occupational types in the
   crowd: the butcher with axe, steel and apron (left foreground), the sweep with
   his brush (centre foreground), the gentleman (right foreground) with long stick
   or wand and erect carriage, and the yeoman farmer with a spade (right
   foreground). This print was reproduced in *The British Antidote*, one of several
   collective volumes directed against George III's favourite, who is here being
   burnt.

The SCOTCH YOKE; or English Resentment.

A New SONG. To the Tune of, *The Queen's ASS.*

OF *Freedom* no longer, let *Englishmen* boast,
Nor *Liberty* more be their favourite Toast;
The *Hydra* OPPRESSION your *Charter* defies,
And galls *English* Necks with the *Yoke* of EXCISE.
The Yoke of Excise, the Yoke of Excise,
And galls English Necks with the Yoke of Excise.

In vain have you conquer'd, my brave Hearts of Oak,
Your *Laurels*, your *Conquests*, are all but a *Yoke*;
Let a r----f----ly PEACE serve to open your Eyes,
And the d--n--ble Scheme of a CYDER-EXCISE.
A Cyder-Excise, a Cyder-Excise,
And the d--n--ble Scheme of a Cyder-Excise.

What though on your *Porter* a Duty was laid,
Your *Light* double-tax'd, and encroach'd on your Trade
Who e'er could have thought that a BRITON so wise,
Would admit such a Tax as the CYDER-EXCISE!
The Cyder-Excise, the Cyder-Excise!
Would admit such a Tax as the Cyder-Excise!

I appeal to the Fox, or his Friend JOHN A BOOT,
If tax'd thus the *Juice*, then how soon may the *Fruit?*
Adieu then to good *Apple-puddings* and *Pyes*,
If e'er they should taste of a cursed EXCISE.
A cursed Excise, a cursed Excise,
If e'er they should taste of a cursed Excise.

Let those at the H------m, who have sought to enslave
A Nation so glorious, a People so brave;
At once be convinc'd that their Scheme you despise,
And shed your last Blood to oppose their EXCISE.
Oppose their Excise, oppose their Excise,
And shed your last Blood to oppose their Excise.

Come on then my Lads, who have fought and have bled
A Tax may, perhaps, soon be laid on your Bread;
Ye Natives of *Worc'ster* and *Devon* arise,
And *strike* at the *Root* of the CYDER EXCISE.
The Cyder-Excise, the Cyder-Excise,
And strike at the Root of the Cyder-Excise.

No longer let K------s at the H--m of the St---e,
With fleecing and grinding pursue *Britain's* Fate;
Let Power no longer your Wishes disguise,
But *off* with their *Heads* --- by the Way of EXCISE.
The Way of Excise, the Way of Excise,
But off with Heads --- by the Way of Excise.

From two *Latin* Words *ex* and *scindo*, I ween,
Came the *hard Word* EXCISE, which *to cut off* does mean,
Take the Hint then, my Lads, let your Freedom advise
And give them a *Taste* of their *fav'rite* EXCISE.
Their fav'rite Excise, their fav'rite Excise,
And give them a Taste of their fav'rite Excise.

Then toss off your Bumpers, my Lads, while you may
To PITT and Lord TEMPLE, Huzza, Boys, Huzza!
Here's the King that to tax his poor Subjects denies,
But Pox o' the *Schemer* that plann'd the EXCISE.
That plann'd the Excise, that plann'd the Excise,
But pox o' the Schemer that plann'd the Excise.

1763.

2. BMC 8681   1 November 1795   Gillray
The Republican Attack
Depicts the damage inflicted on George III's coach as he drove to open
parliament on 29 October 1795, at a period when public discontent was at a
new height. Gillray uses the event to attack opposition politicians, all of whom
are depicted as the ragged Jacobin assailants of the King. They are (from left to
right in the foreground) the Duke of Grafton, Lord Stanhope, the diminutive
Lord Lauderdale, Sheridan, Charles James Fox and Lord Lansdowne.

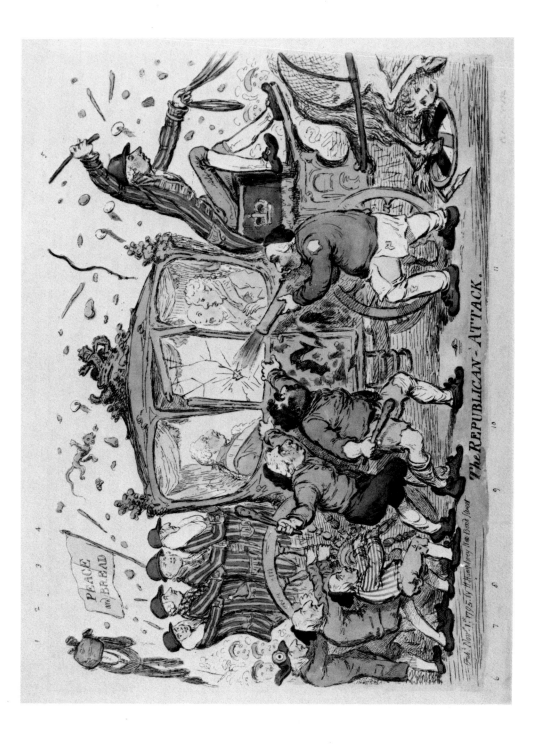

Pub.^d Novr 1.st 1795. by H Humphrey N.º 37 Bond Street

The REPUBLICAN-ATTACK.

3. BMC 524   1726   W. Hogarth
Hudibras Encounters the Skimmington
Hogarth's version of Plate III from the 1726 edition of Samuel Butler's
Hudibras. Depicts the skimmington, a public shaming ritual designed to punish
the violation of domestic and marital norms. Hogarth's print is altogether more
dynamic than Plate 4. The figures are active and sinuous and the form has the
energy and movement of a Renaissance processional painting.

W. Hogarth Inv. et sculp.

4. BMC 441   1710
   Hudibras Encounters the Skimmington
   One of a series of illustrations to the 1710 edition of Butler's *Hudibras*. An
   altogether more pedestrian and static depiction of the shaming ritual. The
   victims are the husband and wife mounted on the horse to the left: he carries a
   distaff and she a ladle with which she appears to be striking her spouse. This
   would seem to indicate that she is being punished as a domineering shrew and
   he as a henpecked husband incapable of exercising authority in his own house.

5. BMC 1392   1708
Third Volume of Mr. T. Brown's Works no. 1
An illustration to a volume that satirises the sights and manners of London, which the author (upper right) shows to a distressed Indian, i.e. native of the West Indies. Books on the sights and ways of the metropolis were a popular genre in the eighteenth century. The street seller with his wheelbarrow full of nuts is typical of a whole series of street sellers, many of whom peddled their wares from carts, barrows and panniers. They 'cried' their goods on the London streets.

The Third Volume of
Mr. T. Browns Works

E. Kn.   M. V. Gu.

6. BMC 1511   1709

Frontispiece to *Crispin Cobler's Confutation of Ben H(oadly)* 3rd ed.

An excellent example of how a tradesman's dabbling in politics is portrayed as having disastrous consequences. The cobbler on the left has so imbibed the ideas of Bishop Hoadly – taken to be those that justify the right of subjects to resist their rulers – that he has lost most of his trade and business. Moreover his son, taking up the same ideas in domestic government, attacks his father with a poker because of his failure to maintain the family. Note the unusually large number of books above the fireplace.

7. BMC 2030   1734
Frontispiece to *The Humours of a Country Election*
Published shortly after the highly controversial election of 1733, the print
shows three stages in a country contest: the candidates arrive in town, they treat
the electors, plying them with food and wine, and they are chaired in triumph
after the poll. The print is crudely executed but successfully conveys the
exuberant, holiday-like spirit of eighteenth-century elections. It also implies that
the candidates are being elected to a borough somewhat like Old Sarum, which
consisted merely of a few cottages and old dwellings.

8. BMC 2332   1737
   The British Hercules
   A British tar depicted as resting in the manner of the Farnese Hercules. The
   classical reference and form lends a dignity to the sailor that is rarely found in
   depictions of the common people. The print is one of many attacks on
   Walpole's reluctance to take military action against the Spanish in the period
   immediately before the outbreak of the War of Jenkin's Ear.

Spithead

I wait for Orders

The British Hercules

1737

9. BMC 3750   1760   Bartho. Warren
St. Monday,   Frontispiece to *Low Life*
A typical cross-section of low life. Note both the coarse features and
occupational stereotypes of the figures portrayed. All of them are shown
neglecting their work for private pleasures on 'Saint' Monday. This was
common practice amongst eighteenth-century artisans and labourers. Figures
include a shoemaker, a tailor (holding shears), a butcher, a farrier and a painter.
Note the disapproving gentleman peering through the window.

St. Monday.

Frontispiece to Low Life.

Bart.o Warren sculp.

Printed for John Lever at Little Moregate next London Wall near Moorfields.

10. BMC 2598   1743
   Doctor Rock's Political Speech to the Mob in Covent Garden
   The device of this print was a popular one in the eighteenth century: to equate
   the quack doctor and seller of patent medicines with the devious politician who
   offered political panaceas to the nation. This attack on a declaimer to a gullible
   mob probably reflects the widespread disillusionment with politics in 1742 after
   Sir Robert Walpole's fall. Many had hoped that the demise of the 'Great Man'
   would produce major changes in politics and the elimination of what they
   regarded as corruption. No such thing occurred.

London Publifhed according to Act of Parliament. Aug.sup27.1743. by G. Foster at the White Horse on Ludgate Hill.

11. BMC 5074   1 July 1772
    The Blacksmith lets his Iron grow cold attending to the Taylor's News
    An *Oxford Magazine* print on the theme of tradesmen neglecting their work for
    politics. Note the vacant looks and ill-formed postures of the figures and the
    portrait of Wilkes on the blacksmith's wall. This print may be a visual reference
    to Joseph Wright of Derby's *The Blacksmith's Shop*, which was first exhibited
    in 1770.

The Blacksmith, lets his Iron grow cold
attending to the Taylor's News.

12. BMC 5086   10 December 1772   Bretherton
The Morning News
A group listen to the latest political news. Note the open-mouthed expression of the figure on the right, and the several signs of disorder: the ramshackle building in the rear, the disorderly dress of the figures on the left and right, and the dog pilfering food – a sign that the tradesmen are negligent.

The Rabble gather round the Man of News

And listen with their mouths

THE MORNING NEWS

Some tell, some hear, some judge of news, some make it.

And he that lyes most loud, is most believ'd. —

Publish'd as the Act directs 10th December 1772. By J. Bretherton No 134 New Bond Street

13. BMC 3085   1750
   Stand Coachman, or the Haughty Lady Well Fitted
   Citizens march through the coach of an arrogant woman who would not move
   and cease obstructing the highway. Note the usual street figures – the squat
   sweep (left foreground), the news seller, and the hairdresser with his wigbox.
   The contrast between the open, public street and the enclosed private coach is
   discussed on p.26. This print is supposedly based on an actual incident.

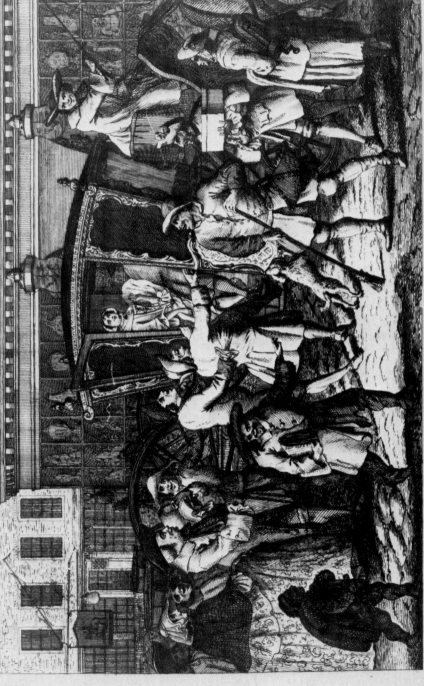

STAND COACHMAN, OR THE HAUGHTY LADY WELL FITTED.

At a Toy Shop hard by Charing Cross tother Day, | But being that Favour most rudely denied, | The Mobb seeing this, they all laughd at the Whim, | The Lady much ruffled, soon alterd her Tone,
A Lady's Coach stood quite across the Foot Way: | By John on the Box, and his Lady beside: | And swore twas as fine for the right as for him. | And call'd to her Coachman in haste to move on:
A Person did civily th'Coachman intreat | The Gentleman, finding that Words would not do, | So hoysting each other, just like a Ships Crew | To tupid the fair Ladies from hence will remove,
To pull up, and let him pass over the Street: | He op'ed the Coach Doors, and genteely went thro' | Buffeteted and dirty, began to march thro' | How they stop a Free Passage with such haughty Air

Taken from Life, and Publish'd according to Act of Parliament, for J. Wakelin in Fleet Street Price 6.d — 1750.

14. BMC 2688   1 April 1745   Hogarth
    Marriage A La Mode, Plate 1
    This print is a complete essay in eighteenth-century social relations. The
    ungainly though prosperous merchant marries off his attractive though
    unsophisticated daughter to the ne'er-do-well son of a finely pedigreed but
    financially ailing aristocrat. Thus begin the famous vicissitudes of the young
    couple.

15. BMC 3260   1753
    The Robin Hood Society
    Shows this famous eighteenth-century debating society that met in Butcher's
    Row, London, and which was frequented by apprentices and tradesmen who
    discussed controversial issues of religion and politics. All the figures depicted
    here are awkward and vulgar, with ungainly postures and foolish faces.

THE ROBIN HOOD.

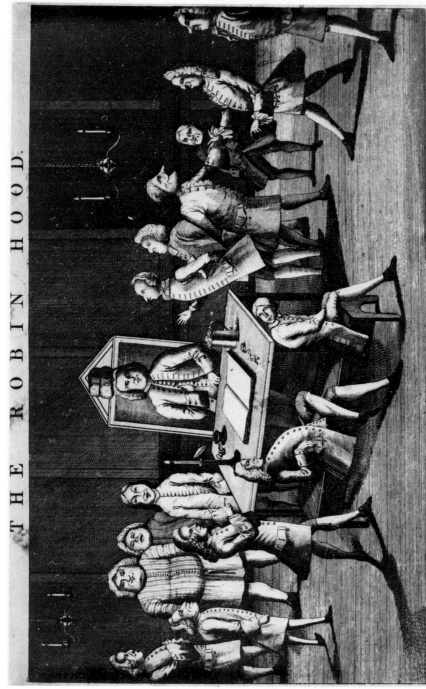

It is impossible to trace the Origin of the above Society; the me imagine they first took the Name of Robin Hood from their Shooting with long Bows, which Custom they still retain: and to deduce them from any particular Nation is equally impossible, for they are composed of every Nation on Earth; we must therefore be content with the following short Description of their present State:— The Number of them is about 300, composed chiefly of Shoe-makers, Apothecaries, Lamp-lighters and Parish-School-Masters &c. a BAKER at their Head for President: they assemble every Monday Evening, when they debate publickly on the most important subjects, as Religion, Politicks and the Moral Funds of Things; and each Member is allowed five Minutes to handle the subject according to his Art; and then the Baker reads up the whole of their Arguments, mixd them with the leaven of his Understanding, and proportions them out into Cakes, according to the Merits of each speaker?

N.B. Should this Account raise any ones Curiosity, they are desired to enquire any Monday Afternoon, near Butcher Row, and their Curiosity may be satisfied for a Pot of Porter.

Mr. CALEB JEACOCKE.

Published according to Act of Parliament June 1 1753.

16. BMC 4113 1765 O'Neale
    Frontispiece to *A Lecture on Heads by the celebrated George Stevens*
    One of the numerous editions of Stevens' *Lecture on Heads*, illustrating some of
    the figures that he satirised in his stage performance or 'lecture'. Note especially
    figure 46, the City Politician, who is portrayed as rotund – a reference to his
    partiality to good food and aldermanic feasts, and as vacant – alluding to his
    political malleability and ignorance.

Frontispeice to the Celebrated Lecture on Heads.

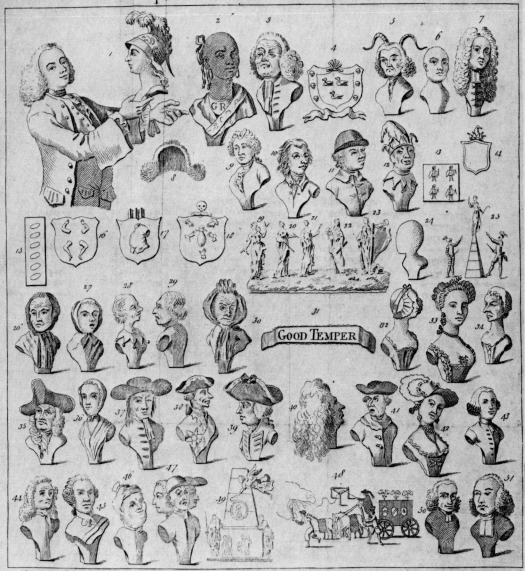

1 Alexander the Great	11 The Jockey	21 Poetry	31 Venus's Girdle	41 The Blood
2 Cherokee Cheif	12 Nobody	22 Astronomy	32 French Night Cap	42 Lady of the Town
3 Quack Docter	13 Four Court Knaves	23 Music	33 New Married Lady	43 Master among the Maids
4 Quack's Arms	14 Nobody's Arms	24 Probability	34 Old Maid	44 The Critic
5 Cuckold	15 A Parcel of Noughts	25 Statute of Flattery	35 Old Batchelor	45 Stock Broker
6 Plain Simple Head	16 Any Body's Arms	26 Riding Hood	36 Maid of the Spirit	46 City Politician
7 Lawyer	17 Some Body	27 Billingsgate Moll	37 The Quaker	47 Gambler's 3 Faces
8 Journeymans Jemmy	18 Every Body's Arms	28 Laughing Philosopher	38 A French Head & Hat	48 Gambler's Funeral
9 Sr Langrish Leaping	19 Architecture	29 Crying Philosopher	39 A English Head & Hat	49 Gambler's Monument
10 The frizzel bob	20 Painting	30 A Head Dress	40 Physical Wigg	50 Tristram Shandy
				51 Methodist Parson

17. BMC 5530   1 November 1778   Robert Dighton
Court of Equity or a Convivial City Meeting
A mezzotint of a meeting or club of London tradesmen and merchants. The Globe in Fleet Street, like many London taverns, was the venue of several clubs which met in private rooms. Such societies were usually convivial, though they also served as business and political associations, as well as providing help to members who found themselves in adversity. This print includes the portrayal of a number of well known London politicians.

18. BMC 3539   1756
Frontispiece to *The Robin Hood Society: A Satire with Notes Variorum by Peter Pounce, Esq; London.*
Another depiction of the Robin Hood Society. Note the interplay of the dogs in the foreground; this is intended to be analogous to the interplay of the debaters and to reflect adversely on the speakers.

19. BMC 3819   9 November 1761
    A View of Cheapside as it appeared on Lord Mayor's Day last
    Lord Mayor's Day in London was both a holiday and a spectacle. In 1761 it
    was also the occasion of a political demonstration against the Scots favourite of
    George III, Lord Bute, and in favour of the recently resigned elder William Pitt.
    Note the royal couple in the draped gallery to the left, the butchers with
    marrow bones and meat cleavers following the mayor's coach, the constables'
    staves to the right and the fallen street seller in the left foreground.

A VIEW of CHEAPSIDE, *as it appeared on* LORD MAYOR's DAY last.

20. BMC 3029   27 April 1749
The British Jubilee being an Exact Representation of the Fire Works in the Green Park at St. James
A celebration after the Peace of Aix-la-Chapelle. Such extravagant firework displays, held to celebrate royal birthdays, national victories, or the end of a war, were not uncommon in the eighteenth century. Note the butchers on the left.

GEORGIVS II REX

THE BRITISH JUBILEE.

View of S.y in Charity.

Being an exact Representation of y.e Fire Works in y.e Green Park at S.t James.   Sold by R. Sayer opposite Fetter-Lane Fleet-Street

21. BMC 9168   3 February 1798   James Gillray
The Loyal Toast
A reference to the celebration of Charles James Fox's birthday – 24 January 1798 – attacking the Duke of Norfolk (figure on the right) for his inflammatory toast. Fox's shadowed jowl can be seen in the centre background as well as such figures as a sweep and a barber with a comb in his hair. The practice of celebrating the birthday of Fox as a Whig anniversary continued well into the nineteenth century.

The LOYAL TOAST.

22. BMC 4018   March 1763
    The Politicians
    Another attack on Lord Bute, the royal favourite, and on the cider tax – an
    extension of the much hated excise tax – and upon the recently signed Peace of
    Paris. One of the large number of prints that comments on the increased interest
    in politics during the 1760s.

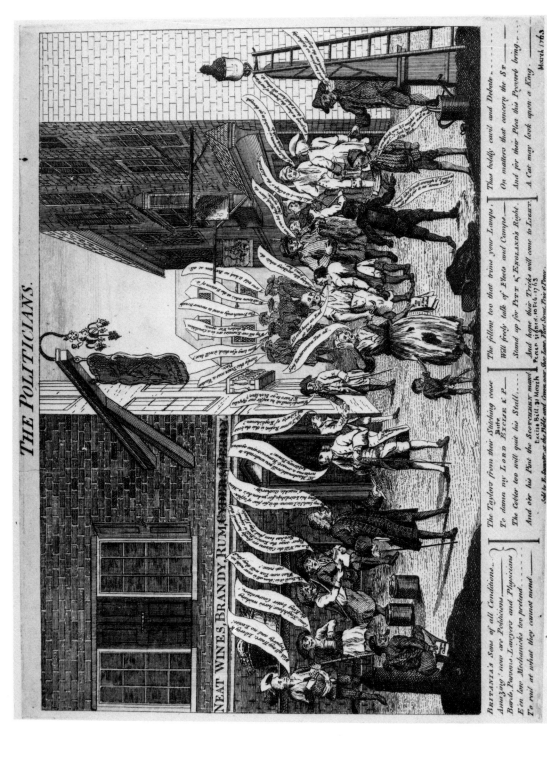

THE POLITICIANS.

23.	BMC 6207 9 April 1783
	An Analysis of Modern Patriotism Performed by Public Opinion & Displayed by Public Indignation
	An attack on Fox's duplicity and his alliance in 1783 with his old enemy, Lord North. Indoors Fox is shown as a supporter of prerogative, while 'out of doors' he continues to act the demagogue, employing his inflammatory opposition rhetoric. Notice Jeffrey Dunstan, Mayor of Garrat (for whom see text and plates 67, 76), deformed and with his wig-bag over his shoulder in the crowd. His pose mirrors that of Fox.

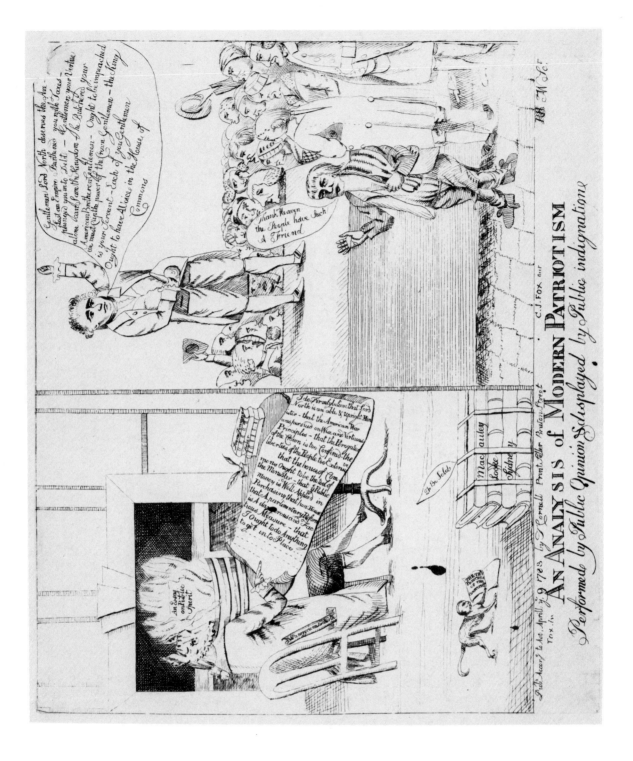

AN ANALYSIS of MODERN PATRIOTISM

Performed by Public Opinion & displayed by Public indignation

24. BMC 9475   1799   Rowlandson
Cries of London, no. 2. Buy my Goose, my fat Goose

CRIES of LONDON. N.º 2.

Buy my Goose, my fat Goose.

London Pub. Jan 1st ... at R. Ackermann's 101 Strand.

25. BMC 9477   1799   Rowlandson
Cries of London, no. 4. Do you want any brickdust
The interaction between the sexes is as important to Rowlandson here as is the subject matter of the aquatint. The pretty girl, the lecherous (usually older) male, and the censorious old woman are stock Rowlandson characters. The sweepers who collected and sold brickdust were amongst the poorest members of the labouring poor.

CRIES of LONDON Nº 4.
Do you want any brick dust.

London Pub Feb 20 1799 at R Ackermann's 101 Strand

26. BMC 9478   1799   Rowlandson
Cries of London, no. 5. Water Cresses, come buy my Water Cresses
The old man entering the brothel and the young creatures leaning from the window provide a moral contrast to the hardworking mother selling cress. Nevertheless the Cry contains a double-entendre.

CRIES of LONDON Nº 5.

Water Cresses, come buy my Water Cresses.

27. BMC 9479   1799   Rowlandson
Cries of London, no. 6. All a growing, a growing, heres Flowers for your Gardens
The amorous implications of the relations between the buyer and seller frame the story of this print.

CRIES of LONDON N.º 6
All a growing, a growing, here's Flowers for your Gardens.
London Pub.d Mar 1, 1799, at R. Ackermann's 101 Strand.

28. BMC 9480   1799   Rowlandson
Cries of London, no. 8. Hot Cross Buns two a penny Buns
Note the parsimony of the clerical figure in the background. This contrasts with
the generous treatment of the children who are given buns.

CRIES of LONDON. Nº 8.
Hot cross Buns two a penny Buns
London Pubd May 4, 1799 at Ackermann's Gallery 101 Strand

29. BMC 2586   2 September 1743
    Discharge of Insolvent Debtors, September 2, 1743
    In the eighteenth century debtors were frequently released from confinement by
    Insolvency Acts passed by parliament. Note the ballad singer on the left, the
    gaoler on the right with his keys, and the young boy in the centre picking a
    gentleman's pocket.

30. BMC 2874   October 1747   J. June
    A Fleet Wedding. Between a brisk young Sailor & his Landlady's Daughter at Rederiff
    A social satire on clandestine marriages which were performed by (usually impecunious) clerics in the Fleet prison or in the surrounding area known as 'the Rules'. Note the usual trades figures – the milkseller, sweep and herbseller. Such marriages as this between a sailor and a whore were stopped by Lord Hardwicke's Marriage Act of 1753, which formalised the civil requirements for a legally binding union.

A FLEET WEDDING.

Between a brisk young Sailor & his Landlady's Daughter at Redcliff.

Scarce had the Coach discharged its trusty Fare, / Pray step this way — Just to the Pen in Hand, / Ill show advancing from the Coaches Side,
But pouring Crouds surround th'amorous Pair: / The Doctor's ready there at your Command: / Till alarmed Parsons quickly hear the Din:
The busy Plyers make a mighty Stir: / The way (another cries) Sir Tal take here / And haste with eothing Words t'invite em in.
And whispering cry, d'ye want the Parson, Sir? / The true and antient Register is Here; / Th'experienced Matron came (an artful Jade)

In this Confusion jostled to and fro, / She led the way without regarding either,
Th'inamour'd Couple know not where to go; / And the first Parson spliced em both together.

Publish'd according to Act of Parliament October y 30th 1747.

Price 6.d
Oct. 1747

31. BMC 2876   December 1747
     Christmass Gambolls. Boxing Day
     There are certain similarities between this print and Plate *19*. Both appear to be
     views of Cheapside from a similar vantage point and perspective. The
     'humours of the city' was a popular literary and visual genre of the eighteenth
     century. It depicted stock characters and situations both to warn and to
     entertain the reader/viewer of these scenes from metropolitan life.

CHRISTMASS GAMBOLLS.

All Sorts of Tracks

First View the Humour of the City,
Judge next if what they do is witty.
Behold that Hero Captain Flash
With empty Pockets cuts a Dash!

Mark Fickle on the other Side,
Shrinks from the Crowd, his Soul kant hide.
Next Doctor Rock and Wellied View.
Preaching sound Doctrine to the Crew.

BOXING DAY
The Beadle in a Rage annews.
M.hurras, Oranges & Frencher Boys.
Throws Halfpence, Our & Barrow, down.
With Barbers Boy, upon the Ground.

The Duke of Limbs and Pegs appear!
Mark how two Punsters at him jeer.
View t'other Part twill make you laugh.
Youd better tag them both by half.

Publish'd according to Act of Parliament Dec.ʳ 26, 1747 by P. Griffin Fleet Street. price 6.ᵈ

32. BMC 2877   1747
The Covt. Garden Morning Frolick. Gaillardise du Commun Jardin
One of several scenes of Covent Garden Revels. Covent Garden was not only
the chief vegetable market in London (see the sellers on the right) but the
location of the city's most famous bagnios and bordellos.

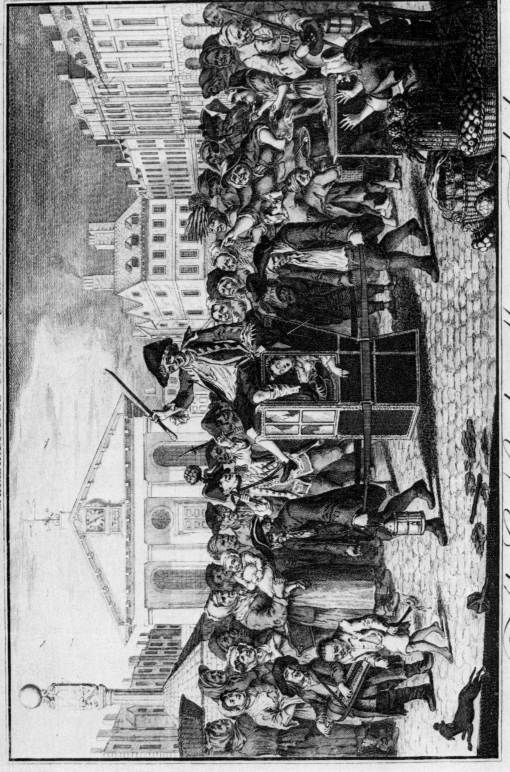

GAILLARDISE du COMMUN JARDIN.

The Cov: Haarden. Morning. Frolick.

33. BMC 3111   c.1750
Greenwich Hill or Holyday Gambols
Greenwich Hill was a popular place for Londoners of all classes to visit and
desport themselves, especially on weekends.

GREENWICH HILL,
or Holyday Gambols.

I re-ecchoed, See who are such of the Sport
And the state lampoon'd Follies of Ballroom or Court,
For t'haunt heart the Madk'er Greenwich resort,

Then heighten'd with Rapture, which never can pall,
You'd own the Debates of Assembly and Ball,
Are as dull as Tonightnot, & just nothing at all.

34. BMC 3076   April 1750

   The Military Prophet: or a Flight from Providence. Address'd to the Foolish and the Guilty, who timidly withdrew themselves on the Alarm of another Earthquake

   This print very effectively both conveys and satirises the sense of panic during the earthquake hysteria of April 1750. After two minor tremors in the previous two months it was widely believed that a more serious earthquake would ensue in April. The clergy used the occasion to urge moral improvement – hence the disreputable character of most of those fleeing the city – and thereby increased public fear. Much of the print's success – its tension – is derived from its highly compressed form.

JACO-INDEPENDO-REBELLO-PLAIDO.

How we're Drest

O hou't spare our Souls for the Gallica king

Mortgang Chest

Warranted dispatched

Who trusta the Pool the Ink

I have the Fee in my Hand

Sinee the Devil his Due

Trentham and Warren

Westminster Hall

D. Bobin Sculp   *17*

1 First Plaid Jac Inc:
2 Height Bubble Parchment 4 Busy body & Constable
3 Busy bustle
  1 Vox Bottom
5 The Dudwicks Teplagh 8 Minuets
7 Mons Trompett &c
6 Guest Reg Tweets

Britons brave are true and unconfind   Fixt to no Party. censure all alike
To lash the Coxcombs of the Age, designd,   And the distinguish'd Villain sure to strike:
Publish'd according to Act of Parliament Feb'y y'e 3'd 1747.

Pleas'd we behold the great maintain the Cause
And court and country join the loud applause.

Price 6'd

36. BMC 2859   27 June 1747
The Humours of the Westminster Election, or the scald miserable Independant Electotors in the Suds
From the same plate as Plate 35, though with substantial alterations. The venue of the print has been changed to the usual place of the Westminster hustings, near St. Paul's, Covent Garden.

37. BMC 2861 1747

The Banker's Election Triumph or a Caution to Moneyd People

An attack on Mr. William Belchier, banker, and M.P. for Southwark. The print condemns Belchier as a parvenu and toady. Note the portrayal of the sailor who runs by the front wheel of Belchier's coach; his figure is similar to those found in prints and paintings that show triumphal processions.

The BANKER's Election TRIUMPH or A CAUTION to Moneyd People.

38. BMC 1539   710
   The Coffeehous Mob, Frontispiece to *The Fourth Part of Vulgus Britannicus: or the British Hudibras*
   Depicts the interior of one of the very large number of coffeehouses (over 500) in London. Newspapers and pamphlets were available to customers and citizens went to the coffeehouse both to read and to discuss the latest news. 1710 was a year of especially vehement controversy because of the Whig party's impeachment of the Tory Dr. Sacheverell for preaching a sermon attacking the Glorious Revolution.

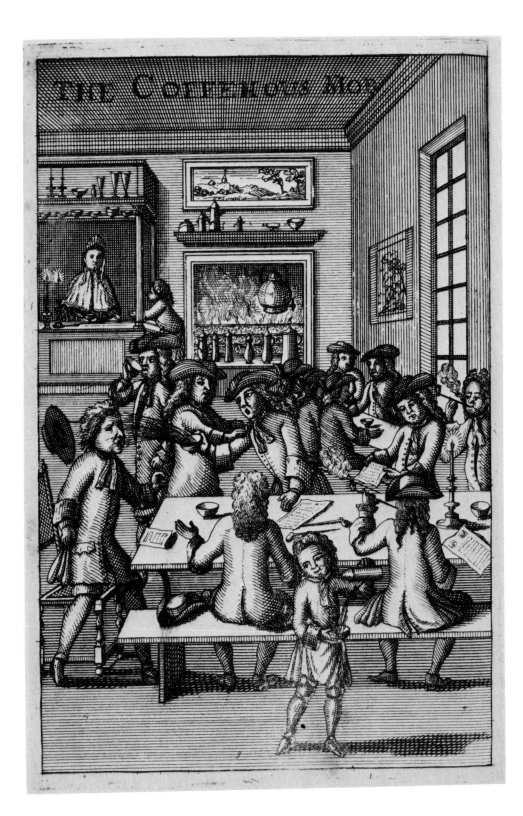

39. BMC 5073   1 April 1772
    Another coffeehouse scene designed to convey the disruptive character of
    politics. Political debate leads the coffee boy to spill his tray, and the informally
    dressed figure on the right to mispour his coffee.

The Coffee-house Politicians.

40. BMC 4190   28 March 1768
The Rape of the Petti-coat

A somewhat static and wooden depiction of an incident in March 1768 when the Lord Mayor, Alderman Harley, together with a group of constables (they can be seen holding their staves of office), seized a Boot and Petticoat on a gibbet outside the Mansion House. The Jack Boot represents *John* Stuart, Earl of *Bute*, the royal favourite, and the petticoat represents the Princess Dowager of Wales, George III's mother and the putative controller of the young king because of her alleged affair with Bute. The Boot and Petticoat were being paraded by a crowd celebrating Wilkes's first election of Middlesex. The actual affray was far more violent than is depicted here. Note the dog fouling Harley's robe.

The Rape of the Petti-coat.

*He valiantly seiz'd the Petti-coat and Boot at the
Portal of his own Mansion.*

Daily adv.

41. BMC 4223   December 1768
   The Brentford Election
   A vivid depiction of the assault on the hustings during the Middlesex by-election of December 1768 by a number of men hired as 'bruisers' by the court candidate, Sir William Beauchamp Proctor. Proctor was defeated by the radical, John Glynn, who was Wilkes's counsel. The print is violently anti-Proctor: it shows Proctor's cronies striking down innocent women and street sellers; in fact, though Proctor's followers began the battle, both sides were implicated in the violence. The poll had to be closed and the election reheld several days later. The print is dynamic in execution, the action extending beyond the boundaries of the print.

Liberty and P...

Bring down the Poll Book I shall betray'um

D—n ye you does well that Grou you all persuade

42. BMC 4226   December 1768
An Election Entertainment at Brentford
Politics as disorder in the context of the Middlesex by-election of December
1768. Such electoral 'treating' was commonplace, though overt bribery was less
usual. This is another pro-Glynn and anti-Proctor print. Notice the role played
by animals in the print – they are all symbols of neglect and disorder – and the
remarkable, almost aristocratic pose of the butcher who refuses a bribe.

An Election Entertainment at Brentford.

43. BMC 4937   1 January 1772
   Quidnunc, or the Upholsterer Shaving
   A satire, based on Arthur Murphy's play, *The Upholsterer, or What News?*,
   which satirised the political obsessions of Quidnunc, the Upholsterer, and
   Roger, the barber. The political allusion is to the London sheriff's election of
   1771 at which the radical John Wilkes and his ally, Frederick Bull, were elected.
   Note the cats spoiling the wig in the foreground.

Quid nunc, or the Upholdsterer Shaving.

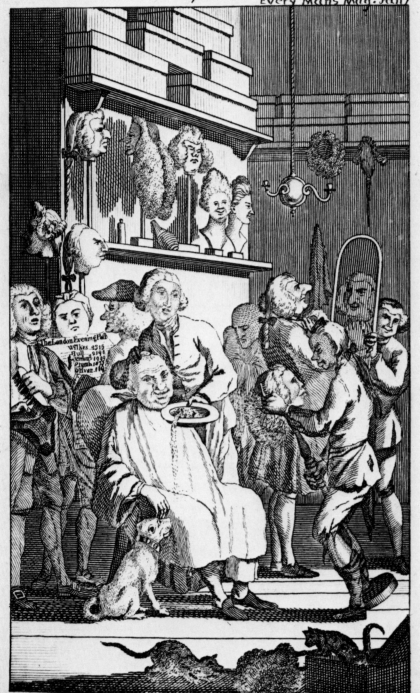

The London Evening Post
Wilkes. 4315
Hull 2141
Hersat 1919
Plumb 1079
Oliver 110

44. BMC 5665   8 May 1780

    A Petitioning, Remonstrating, Reforming, Republican

    The earliest really hostile portrayal of a humble reformer, much more in the
    spirit of the 1790s than of the 1780s. Notice the tattered and torn clothing of
    the republican, a sign of general disorder.

A Petitioning. Remonstrating. Reforming. Republican.

Liberty & Rebellion

YOUR PETITIONER SHEWETH,

That he Humbly wishes to

Reduce y.^e Church to Gospel Order
By Rapine Sacrilege & Murther
To make Presbyty supream
& Kings themselves submit to him

& not content all this to do
He must have Wealth & Honor too
Or else with Blood & desolation
He'll tear it out of the Heart of the nation

8 May. 1780

Publ.^d acc.^o to Act. May.e. 1780 by M.Darly 39 Strand.

45. BMC 5776   1 January 1780   W. Austin
Public Ordinary
A satire on a feast at a Militia Camp. Note the dog stealing the food. The figure chucking the serving wench under the chin is Wilkes, who was a colonel in the Buckinghamshire militia.

Public Ordinary.

London, Published as the Act Directs Jan. 1799. Oh what a charming thing a being. By Robert Wilkinson at N.°58 in Cornhill.

46. BMC 7637   March 1790
   A Dissenting Congregation
   An attack on Protestant dissenters. Note the dilapidated building, the dog
   fouling a paper inscribed 'Repeal of Corporat(ion) & Test Act', and the sour
   and grim expressions of the congregation. Dissenters were disparaged as
   supporters of the radical principles of the French Revolution, and their attempt
   to secure the repeal of the Test and Corporation Acts, which imposed certain
   civil disabilities on dissenters, was not given a sympathetic hearing.

47. BMC 8729   12 August 1796   J. Nixon
Frontispiece to *Ode to the Hero of Finsbury Square*
An attack on the social pretensions of James Lackington who opened the first
London book emporium specialising in cheap editions and remainders, an
enterprise that made him a fortune. Note the use of the coach as a symbol of
conspicuous consumption, the dog defecating on Lackington's *Memoir* and the
crude expressions of the crowd that includes a butcher and a barber's boy.

SMALL PROFITS
DO
GREAT THINGS

CHEAPER than any Bookseller in the World

PUFFS & LIES for my Book

COMMON PRAYER

TILLOTSON

I. Lackington   Bookseller   Frontis. to Ode to the Hero of Finsbury Square by Peregrine Pindar

1795

48. BMC 4280   22 March 1769
The Battle of Temple Bar
Depicts the London mob's attack on anti-radical merchants seeking to deliver a loyal address to George III. Notice how the action spills out beyond the edge of the print. The scene is Temple Bar, the gate that marked the boundary between the cities of London and Westminster. Broadsides, newspapers and prints were often attached to it for public view, as can be seen in the print.

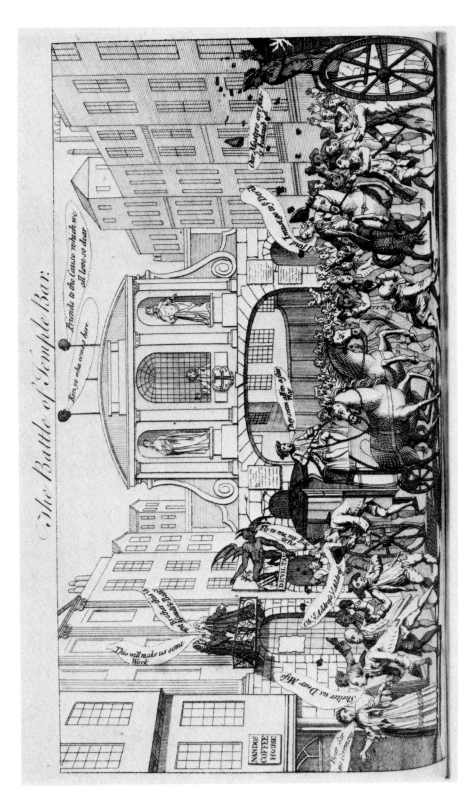

The Battle of Temple Bar.

49. BMC 4281   March 1769
   Sequel to the Battle of Temple Bar
   The scene outside St. James' Palace when the remnants of the merchant
   procession seen in Plate *48* finally arrived at the Royal Palace. Note St. James'
   Coffee House, the leading Whig coffeehouse, on the right, and the elaborate
   hearse commemorating the deaths of two men, one killed by troops outside the
   King's Bench prison during the so-called St. George's Fields Massacre of May
   1768, the other killed during the affray at the December Middlesex by-election
   seen in Plate *41*. The coach was driven by Lord Mountmorris, an aristocratic
   supporter of Wilkes.

SEQUEL to the Battle of TEMPLE BAR.

50. BMC 4852   10 April 1771

An Exact Representation of the Seven Malefactors that where executed at Tower Hill on April, 1771 F(or Treason) to their Country

This bold print depicts the ritual execution of seven effigies of leading enemies of the radicals and Wilkites which took place on April Fools Day, 1771, and again a few days later. The effigies were ritually decapitated by a chimney sweep. The publisher of this print, John Williams, had been in the pillory for publishing the collected edition of John Wilkes' *North Briton*. The mock execution was organised by William Penrice, a former turnkey in the King's Bench Prison, and by a London publican. They hired coffins and carts for the occasion.

An exact representation of the seven Malefactors that where executed at Tower Hill on April 5 1771 for Tomson to their Country.

51. BMC 5684   1 July 1780

The Burning and Plundering of Newgate & Setting the Felons at Liberty by the Mob

One of several prints of the most dramatic event of the Gordon Riots in London of 1780. All of the London prisons were thrown open and several of them damaged, though none more extensively than the felons' gaol at Newgate. For the riot see p.28 and plates 52, 53 and 90. The disorders after the presentation to parliament of the Protestant Association's petition against Catholic Relief lasted for more than a week, caused extensive property damage, and led to the deaths of 285 rioters during the riots and the execution of 25 more. The event was a major trauma for the London radicals, some of whom favoured and some of whom opposed Catholic Relief, and all of whom were dismayed by the street violence.

The Burning & Plundering of NEW GATE & Setting the Felons at Liberty by the Mob.

Published 1 July 1781 by Fielding & Walker, Pater Noster Row.

52. BMC 5686   June 1780   Hamilton
The Devastations occasioned by the Rioters of London firing the New Gaol of
Newgate, and burning Mr. Akerman's furniture &c June 6 1780
A second print of the pyrotechnics outside the Newgate Gaol.

London Published by Alex'r Hogg at the King's Arms N° 16 Paternoster Row.

A The prisoners in irons in each apartment were released thro' the walls

The Devastations occasioned by the RIOTERS of LONDON Firing the New Goal of NEWGATE, and burning M.r Akerman's Furniture, &c. June 6. 1780.

Thornton sculp.

Smithes delin.

53. BMC 5844   10 July 1781   H. Roberts
An Exact Representation of the Burning, Plundering and Destruction of
Newgate by the Rioters on the memorable 7th of June 1780
The last and most effective representation of the event. There is a strong sense
of turmoil and action, heightened by the large number of intersecting lines made
by the staves and bludgeons.

An Exact Representation of the Burning, Plundering and Destruction of NEWGATE by the Rioters, on the memorable 7th. of June 1780.

London Published as the Act directs, July 20th. 1781, by J. Mackett, North Audley Street, Grosvenor Square and J. Fielding No. 23 Pater Noster Row.

54. BMC 4259   1768?   T. Stayner after Collett
A Taylor riding to Brentford
An attack on both the social and political aspirations of the humble. The tailor riding to Brentford must have been a very successful subject as it was also the title of one of the first comic equestrian acts at the first English circus, Astley's, which was held in a building at the foot of Westminster Bridge.

A TAYLOR riding to BRENTFORD.

Engraved from an Original Picture Painted by Mr. John Collett.

55. BMC 5613   30 July 1779
   A Meeting of City Politicians
   Artisan gatherings such as this were common in London taverns and were much
   remarked upon by foreign visitors to the metropolis. A characteristically
   pejorative portrayal whose technique emphasises the vulgarity of the subjects.

PLATE 2. OF EVERY THING HUMOROUS, RIDICULOUS, AND SATYRICAL.

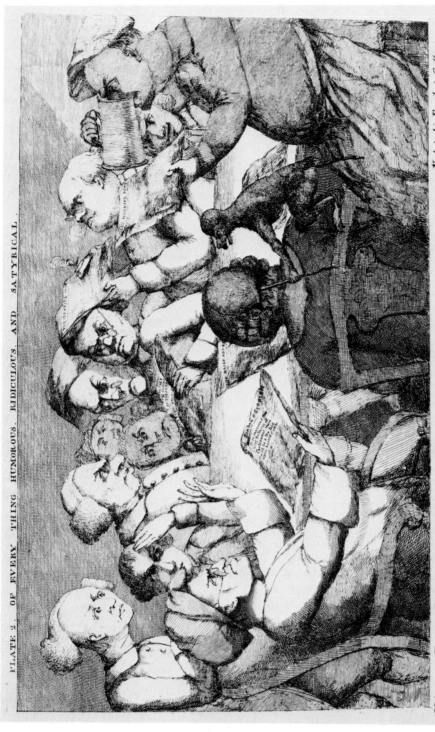

With staring Eye, & open Ear,   Neglects his Family & Calling.
Each catching Horrid Hy-over, A MEETING OF CITY POLITICIANS. To enter into Party Branding.
Swallows down Politics with Beer.   Gets Drunk & Swears — the Ninnies falling

Published July 30th 1779 by Wm Richardson. No 68 High Holborn.

56. BMC 6500   5 April 1784   J. Boyne
    The Political Beggar
    This print refers to a low point in Fox's fortunes during the famous
    Westminster election of 1784 which he eventually won, defeating a former
    political ally who had gone over to the court. The print exploits Fox's usually
    unkempt appearance, including the shadow of his beard (hence he was called
    'Blackbeard'), and his propensity to 'dress down'.

Publish'd Aprill 5 1784   by H. Mac'Phail N.º 62 High Holborn.

THE POLITICAL BEGGAR,

I am Grown so Unfashionable that Dogs bark at me as I halt by them

57. BMC 6624   22 June 1784   J. Barrow?
The Mumping Fox or Reynard turn'd Beggar
A reference to Fox's use of a public subscription to pay for the costs of the
electoral scrutiny after the extremely expensive Westminster election of 1784.
All of the pejorative associations with the word Fox are used here. Note the
butchers in the right background (they were portrayed as ardent supporters of
Fox and the amorous companions of the Duchess of Devonshire, his leading
female aristocratic supporter). They are accompanied by Sam House, the
publican, for whom see p.34 and plates *69, 70*.

The MUMPING FOX or REYNARD turn'd BEGGAR.

22. June 1784

Politic Reynard here in Statuquo
Displays at once his poverty & woe
Your kind assistance is his only plea
That he may stand the fatal Scrutiny
His Wits you'll find your Pockets is to fleece
Beware ye ganders and beware ye Geese
The Widows mite he'll take between his Crutches
With as much Glee as he would kiss a Dutchess.

Mr Fox

58. BMC 6994   25 November 1786   J. Boyne
Employment During Recess
An attack on Fox (left panel) and Edmund Burke (right). Each is portrayed as a type from the Street Cries of London (see plates *24–8*). The axe that Fox sharpens on his grindstone alludes to the punishment for traitors, and is a reference to the impeachment, led by the Foxite Whigs, of Warren Hastings, the Governor General of India. Burke was the leading Foxite prosecutor of Hastings. The use of the form derived from the Cries of London probably refers to the way in which the Whigs made the trial into a public political forum.

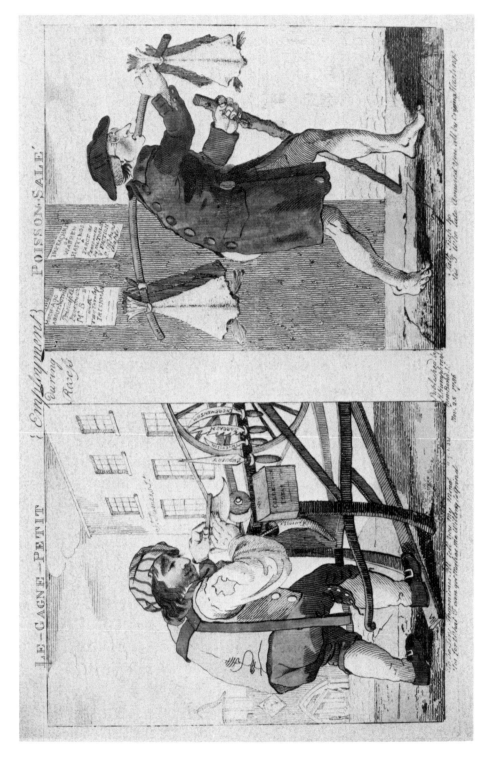

59. BMC 7352 July 1788 Gillray
The Butchers of Freedom
A vicious satire on the Foxites in the Westminster by-election of 1788 in which their candidate, Lord John Townshend (the central figure trampling on a royal navy banner), opposed the re-election of Admiral Hood, one of Fox's opponents in 1784. Fox (defacing the King's Head), George Hanger (with three plumes of the Prince of Wales in his hat), Burke, Sheridan and Lord Derby are all shown as brutal butchers attacking constables (far right) and pro-Hood sailors outside a Hood tavern in Covent Garden. This is an especially good example of the portrayal of gentlemen in plebeian costume as a means of denigrating them.

The BUTCHERS of FREEDOM.

Pub.d July 14 1788 by H. Humphrey New Bond St.

Price 1. s

60. BMC 9022   15 June 1797

A Battle out of the House; or, the Best Way of Settling the Dispute
Fox fights the younger Pitt before an enthusiastic pro-Fox mob. Probably an
anti-Foxite print that emphasises the lowly character of his support. A wide
range of trades is portrayed, each man using language and metaphors
appropriate to his calling. The title of the print probably refers to the decision of
the Foxite opposition to secede from the House of Commons as a means of
protesting against Pitt's government.

A Battle out of the House; or, the Best Way of settling the Dispute!

61. BMC 9180   1 March 1798   Gillray
Consequences of a Successful French Invasion no. 1 Plate 1st.
The first print in a series subsidised by Sir John Dalrymple which, somewhat
surprisingly, was not a commercial success. The print shows the government
benches (on left) crowded with chained convicts, the opposition benches (right)
filled with serried ranks of French soldiers. Sheridan, as a cobbler (centre
foreground) burns the records of liberty, while Fox (on right) depicted as a
blacksmith, destroys the mace. The message is obvious: the success of French
ideas would mean the destruction both of English political institutions and of
English liberty.

Sir John Dalrymple inv.   London, Pub. March 1st 1798, by J. Gillray, Nº 27 St James's Street.—Price 3s. Coloured 1st Nº 39   J. Gillray fecit.

Consequences of a Successfull French Invasion.— Nº I. Plate.1st "We come to recover your long lost Liberties."— Scene The House of Commons.

Description.— One French Soldier putting Hand-cuffs and
another Fetters on the Speaker, whose Mouth is gagged
with a Drawfish. The rest of the Members, two & two, tied
together by the Arms with Cords, (Mr Pitt & Mr Dundas by the
Leg with an Iron Chain, which has three Padlocks, but the Key-
holes spiked up) They are all dressed in the Uniform of the
Convicts of Botany-Bay, to wit, Coats of two Colours, long
Breeches, no Stockings, & their Heads close shaved. French
Guards opposite to the Members with their Hats on. one of

whom carries an Axe, & a Besom of Deaths Head
on his Breast. Two Clerks near him with their Pens in
their Ears, hanging their Heads. Republicans in the
Galleries waving their Hats in which are triple-coloured
Cockades, & clapping their Hands. An English Blacksmith, in his Waistcoat & Cap of Liberty, breaking &
Mace in pieces with a fore Hammer. the Statutes tum-
bled on the Floor. the Cap of Liberty raised high behind the Speakers Chair. below which is painted

in Capital Letters. "This House adjourned to Botany Bay
"fine die". Two Chaffers & burning Charcoal containing to
to stand in their present places in the House, but filled with Red-
hot Irons, to fear the Cheek of the Members before they set
off: & the other, if they shall be found Guilty by the Verdict
of a French Jury, of returning to their own Country without
Leave of the French Directory in Writing. An English Cobler
in the Cap of Liberty raised high be- blowing with a Bellows one of the
Chaffers the Fuel, the Journals of the House.

62. BMC 9039   24 November 1797   Gillray
Le Coup de Maitre
Fox as a singularly unkempt and hirsute Jacobin, assassinating King, Lords and Commons. Gillray ironically dedicates the print to the London Corresponding Society (for which see Plate *91*), the largest of the many artisan radical societies scattered throughout the nation.

Le Coup de Maitre. — This Print copied from the French Original, is dedicated to the London Corresponding Society.

63. BMC 9438   8 July 1799   Gillray
'Elegance Democratique'. A Sketch found near High-Wycombe
Though Lord Wycombe, here portrayed by Gillray, was neither a radical nor
especially politically active, his dress is described as 'democratique' not simply
because of its eccentricity but because it is a good instance of an aristocrat
dressing down. His garb is much closer to that of a Buckinghamshire farmer
than of a member of the House of Lords.

Pub. July 8. 1799 by H. Humphrey, 27 S. James's Street

J. Gilray del. et.

" *ELEGANCE DEMOCRATIQUE*." – a Sketch found near High Wycombe

"– whenever I wish to form a proper estimate of a mans Mind, I observe his Manners & his Dress."

Lord C.

64. BMC 7644   1 May 1790
   A Demosthenean Attitude
   A print of Fox's oratorial manner which draws an analogy between his style of speaking – which was rapid, passionate, unplanned and sometimes disorganised – and his dress. Fox looks like an unkempt plebeian – his hair is dishevelled, his stockings wrinkled and falling, his shoes unfastened. His posture is also totally graceless and unaristocratic.

Publish'd as the Act directs, by Bentley & C.º May 1.º 1790.

A Demosthenean Attitude.

65. BMC 9548   13 October 1800   Gillray
The Worn-out Patriot; or The Last Dying Speech of the Westminster Representative
A satire on the anniversary celebration on 10 October 1800 of Fox's first election to the constituency of Westminster in 1780. Fox is portrayed as bloated, overweight, with legs swollen and a coarse face that registers despair. In the background the typical sweep and butcher, who appear so often as Fox's audience in Gillray's prints, are to be found. The title, with its reference to 'Last Dying Speech', implies both that Fox will shortly die and that he is a criminal – capital felons usually had their 'Last Dying Speech' published at the time of their execution.

Vive la Liberté

"Gentlemen,
———— You see I'm grown quite an Old Man in your Service! Twenty Years I've served you, & always upon the same Principles; I rejoiced at the Succefs of our Enemies in the American War! & the War against the Virtuous French Republic, has always met with my most determind opposition! but the Infamous Ministry will not make Peace with our Enemies, & are determind to keep Me out of their Councils & out of Place! therefore Gentlemen, as their Principles are quite different from mine, & as I am now too Old to form myself according to their System, my attendance in Parliament is usels: & to say the truth, I feel that my season of action is past, & I must leave to younger Men to Act, for alas! my failings & Weaknesses will not let me now recognize what is for the best!

Petition to y Throne! or a new way to Combe the Minister Wig

Whitbread Entire

Publish'd October 13 1800, by H Humphrey 27 St James's Street

The WORN-OUT PATRIOT: ——or—— The Last Dying Speech of the
Westminster Representative, at the Anniversary Meeting on Oct. 10th 1800. held at the Shakspeare Tavern

66. BMC 6117   17 December 1782   T. Colley
Perdito & Perdita – or – the Man & Woman of the People
An extraordinarily coarse and ill-shaven Fox slumps in the famous carriage of
Mrs. Robinson, the former mistress of the Prince of Wales and the current
amour of the 'champion of the people'. The fact that she drives is taken to mean
that she controls the relationship. Mrs. Robinson, daughter of the captain of a
whale ship, actress, author and spouse of an articled clerk, was a beauty who
had alliances with the Prince, Fox and Captain Tarleton. Her elaborately
decorated chariot was notorious, as were her flamboyant styles of dress. She
died an impoverished cripple at the age of 43.

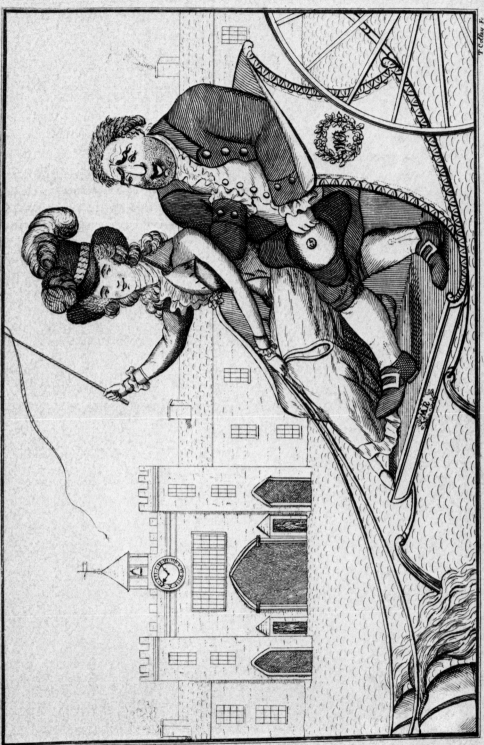

" I have now not fifty ducats in the World & yet I am in love."

Perdito & Perdita — or —— the Man & Woman of the People

Pub.d by W.Richardson N.° 68.High Holborn Dec.r 17.1782.

67. BMC 6331   25 May 1783
The Robin Hood Society
Shows Jeffrey Dunstan, mock mayor of Garrat (see p.33), speaking before
the Robin Hood Society (for which see plates *15, 18*). Dunstan has his wig-bag
over his shoulder and is shown in his usual posture with one hand extended like
the street-crier that he was. Though the print is clearly intended to satirise the
political aspirations of the vulgar – look at the faces of Dunstan's audience – the
motion on the chairman's lectern has a certain sense: August 1st refers to the
date of the Hanoverian succession, Westminster Bridge to the House of
Commons. The motion, therefore, raises the question of the relationship
between King and Commons, a highly topical issue in May 1783.

Q? to be DEBATD
next Thursday Eve
"HOW FAR is it
from the 1 of Aug?
to the foot of:
WESTMINSTER BRIDGE

The ROBIN HOOD SOCIETY.

68. BMC 5877   September 1780   Gillray(?)
Sir Toby Thatch, Candidate for Garret
One of the candidates for the much publicised 1781 mock election at Garrat. Thatch, as is indicated by the tankard on the table, is portrayed drinking at the hostelry of Sam House (see Plates 69, 70) which was in Wardour Street.

SIR TOBY THATCH, CANDIDATE for GARRET.
Jocando Bibendo Vivimus.
His Cytere.

London Published Feby 12. 1795. by Cartwright Berwick Street

69. BMC 5696   1 September 1780   Rowlandson
Samuel House
The boisterous publican, republican and supporter of Fox, dressed in his usual
eccentric manner – no coat, no wig, untied breeches etc. Note the inscription
'No Pope' on the barrel behind House, a reference to the Protestant
Association's activities in 1780, the year of the Gordon Riots.

Samuel House,

the first Man, who jumped off Westminster bridge.

he was a well known Partizan of Mr Charles Fox in Westminster.

Pub'd According to Act Sept 1 1780 by I Jones at No 103 Wardour Street Soho

70. BMC 5697   18 September 1780   T. Rowlandson
Sr Samuel House
A copy of Plate 69. The chief difference is the new inscription on the barrel –
'Fox for Ever. Huzza', referring to the 1780 Westminster election, during which
House worked as a Foxite organiser.

Sr. SAMUEL HOUSE.

Pub.ᵈ According to Act Sepᵗ.ʳ 18 1780 by I. Rowlandson & I. Jones at N.ᵒ 103 Holborn

Warm Partisan of C.J.Fox in Westminster.

10 Sep. 1780

71. BMC 6524   12 April 1784
    The Chairing of Fox
    A pro-Fox election print, showing Fox being carried in triumph by his female
    supporters (including the Duchess of Devonshire in the centre) after his
    successful election for Westminster in 1784. Note Sam House in the left
    background.

Friends freemen Britons all your strength be tried
To quell oppression stem corruptions tide

Let shouting plaudits fill resounding air
And Fox & virtue set in freedoms chair

Pub.^d April 12th 1784 by W. Wall N.° 36 Charles S.^t oppos.^{te} Middlesex Hospittal

S. House.   L.^y Archer   C.J. Fox.   D.^{fs} Devonshire

72. BMC 6564   30 April 1784   Rowlandson
Procession to the Hustings after a Successful Canvass, no. 14
One of a series of prints of the Westminster election year of 1784 executed by
Rowlandson and subsequently reissued in *The History of the Westminster
Election*. This print is typical of Rowlandson's election prints in that it is as
much concerned with social and sexual as with political matters. There is a
tension between the three aristocratic women in the foreground, led by the
Duchess of Devonshire, and the demotic butchers and House in the
background.

KEY OF THE
BACK STAIRS

Tax on
Maid Servants

AND THE RIGHTS
OF THE COMMONS

MAN OF
THE PEOPLE

London Published April 30 1784 by G Humphrey No 48 Long Acre

PROCESSION TO THE HUSTINGS AFTER A SUCCESSFUL CANVASS.

73. BMC 6590   20 May 1784
The Disappointed Candidate Solus!!
The defeated opponent of Fox, Sir Cecil Wray, bitterly looks on as Fox is carried in triumph by his supporters. Note the facade of St. Paul's, Covent Garden which appears in many of the Westminster election prints, and House who is immediately behind a laurel-wreathed Fox.

The DISAPPOINTED CANDIDATE SOLUS !!

I am Bit. D—n the Fox. the D—ſs. Chelsea Hospital. Maid Servants.
Small Beer. the back Stairs. & all together. to be Sure I'm no Speaker I've no Head
I Shall not be brought in but the Scrutiny His M—y will have that
and that Bald Pated Son of a B—h Sam H—se not content
with giving my Opponent Plumpers Threatned to give me
A Plumper in each EYE if I did not Cock my HAT t'other Way.

Pub.d as the Act directs May 20 1784 by W.Humphrey
N.º 227 Strand

74. BMC 6600   26 May 1784   Phillips
The May Garland
A burlesque of the Foxite victory celebration of May 1784 after the
Westminster contest. Note the satiric attacks on Fox's aristocratic female
support ('Petticoat for Ever' and 'Sacred to Female Patriotism'), on his rough
allies – especially the butchers in the centre foreground, and the general
atmosphere of a plebeian saturnalia. The coffin carried in the right foreground
probably refers to the death of one Casson, a constable who was killed in an
affray with a group of Foxite butchers and chairmen. Sam House leads the band
of cleaver-carrying butchers.

THE MAY GARLAND
or Triumph without Victory —

Published by S. Forres N.º 3 Piccadilly May 26 1784

See the Godlike youth advance
Sports prepare and lead the dance
C.J.Fox

Fetes prepare and laurels bring
Songs of triumph to him sing
D.ᵉ Devonshire

Sam House.

Perdition to Sardinia's & High Bailiffs

Marrow bones & Cleavers Constitutional Supporters

Tree of Good & Evil

Succefs to Female Patriotism

75. BMC 6586   18 May 1784   Rowlandson
The Westminster Deserter Drum'd out of the Regiment
A Rowlandson print of House drumming Sir Cecil Wray, the renegade Foxite,
away from the Westminster hustings in 1784. The Chelsea Pensioners with their
crutches and the maidservants with their mops refer to two accusations levelled
at Wray: that he planned to close the Chelsea Hospital and to introduce a tax
on maidservants.

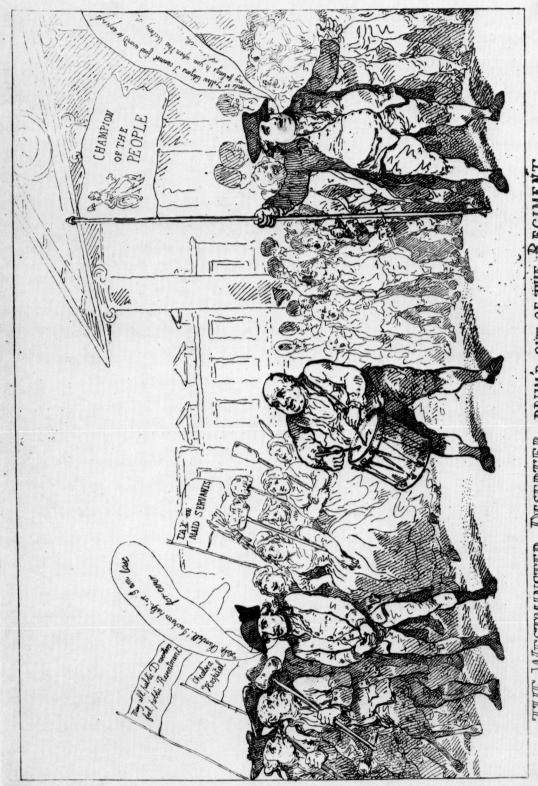

THE WESTMINSTER DESERTER DRUM'D OUT OF THE REGIMENT.

76. BMC 6423   c. Feb. 1784
Mr Fox addressing his Friends from the King's Arms Tavern
House and Dunstan (right) and a collection of characters derived from Street
Cries listen to Fox's speech from the window of the King's Arms. This print
refers to an incident that took place after Fox had been humiliated earlier in the
evening at a meeting in Westminster Hall, where his coalition with Lord North
had been roundly denounced. The print implies that Fox has lost the respectable
support of the Westminster electors and has had to turn to the common mob.

FRONTISPIECE

M^r. Fox addressing his Friends from the King's Arms Tavern Feby 14. 1784.

77.　BMC 6479　31 March 1784
A Sally from Sam's or F–x Canvassing
An attack on Fox and his humble supporters led by Sam House. Fox advances
bearing the jaw bone of an ass – like Samson who smote the Philistines. The
reference is to Fox's rhetorical abilities (hence House's remark, 'He'll tip them
his jaw'), though the implication that the ass's jaw is also Fox's is hardly
complimentary. Note the foxes' brushes carried by House, and worn in the hats
of two rather disreputable supporters.

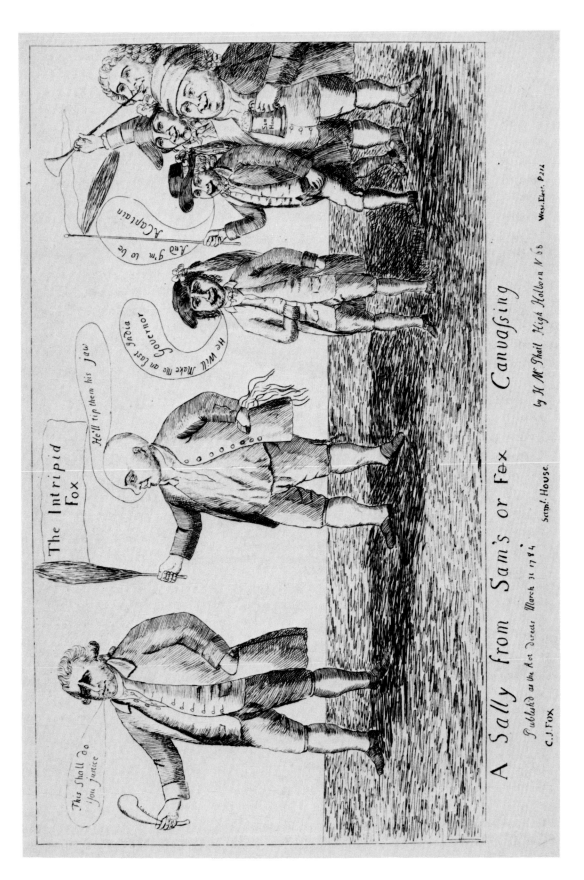

A Sally from Sam's or Fox Canvassing

Publish'd as the Act directs. March 31. 1784.

by H. M.Phail High Holborn N.56.

West. Elect. P.214.

78. BMC 6548   22 April 1784   Rowlandson
Wit's Last Stake or the Cobling Voters and Abject Canvassers
House, Fox and the Duchess of Devonshire portrayed by Rowlandson as
desperate canvassers towards the end of the Westminster election. The print
again alludes to the poverty and therefore the ineligibility of many of those who
voted for Fox. House treats a street scavenger to a mug of ale, while the
Duchess pays a substantial sum for trival shoe repairs in one of the poorest
parts of the city.

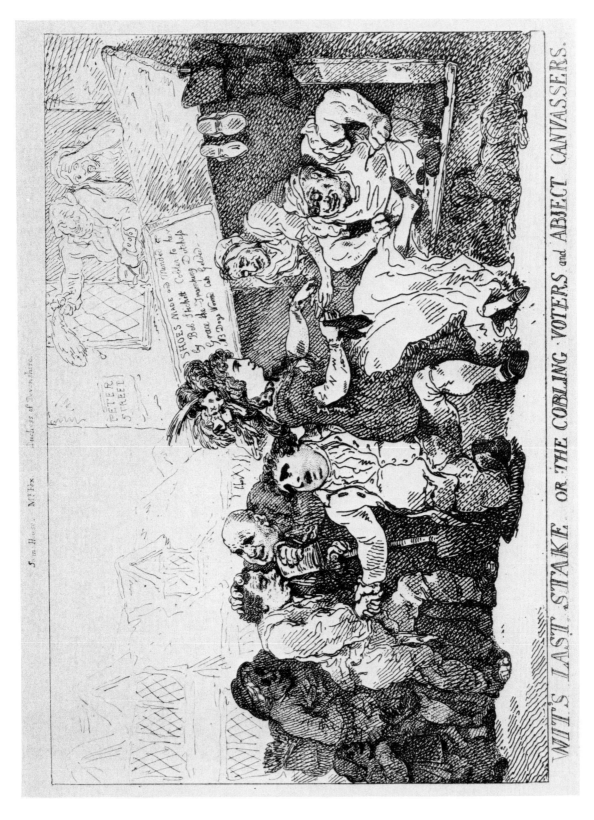

WIT'S LAST STAKE, OR THE COBLING VOTERS and ABJECT CANVASSERS.

79   BMC 6487   1 April 1784
     The Election Tate á Tate
     A print that appeared on the first day of the poll of the Westminster election.
     House and the Duchess of Devonshire appear almost as mirror images, even
     though they represent opposites.

The Election Tate á Tate

Publish'd as the Act directs April 1, 1784 by T. Hartingman, N° 1 New Bond S°

80. BMC 6593   21 May 1784   W. Dent
   The Fox and Geese Triumphant
   Another satirical version of Fox's electoral triumph, showing a mix of
   aristocrats and humble supporters of Fox who here rides on a goose with the
   head of the Prince of Wales. The procession consists of a Westminster justice of
   the peace, Apothecary Hall (a tradesman very active in Fox's cause), the
   diminutive Lord John Cavendish, the Earl of Surrey (an aristocratic republican
   and notorious toper), the Duchess of Devonshire and Sam House.

THE FOX AND GEESE TRIUMPHANT.

21 May 1784.

81. BMC 6536   16 April 1784
A Scene at the New Theatre Covent Garden
Politics as spectacle. The hustings of the 1784 Westminster election. Note the ragged figure on crutches who votes for Fox (centre foreground) and the Duchess of Devonshire and Sam House at opposite ends of the hustings, framing the three candidates Wray, Hood and Fox.

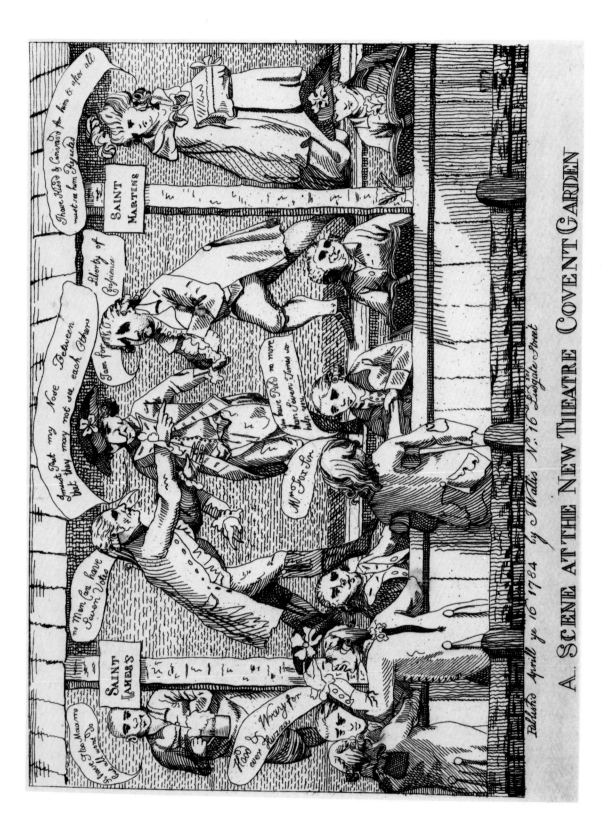

A SCENE AT THE NEW THEATRE COVENT GARDEN

Publish'd April ye 16 1784 by I Wallis No 16 Ludgate Street

82. BMC 6529 Rowlandson
   Lords of the Bedchamber
   House entertained by Fox and the Duchess of Devonshire in her 'bedchamber'.
   The print both titillates – it implies that both Fox and House know the Duchess
   in a compromising fashion – and reassures, for House is shown as adoring, and
   by analogy with the dog (right, centre foreground) as tame or a pet.

Pub. April 4. 1784 by W. Humphrey N 227 Strand

LORDS OF THE BEDCHAMBER.

83. BMC 6527   13 April 1784   W. Dent
   The Duchess Canvassing for her Favourite Member
   The Duchess of Devonshire, with her hand beneath a butcher's apron,
   canvassing for votes. One of the most explicit prints attacking the Duchess's
   willingness to kiss tradesmen as a means of getting votes. Note the venue of this
   assignation – Cockspur Street – and the reference to the butcher's 'Plumper'.

THE DUTCHESS CANVASSING FOR HER FAVOURITE MEMBER.

84. BMC 6541   20 April 1784   W. P. Carey
The Devonshire Minuet, danced to Ancient British Music through
Westminster, during the present Election
Another satire on the Duchess's activities as a canvasser for Fox during the
Westminster election. Note the contrast between the delicate features of the
Duchess and the coarse forms of the butchers. 'Ancient British Music' refers to
the butchers' practice of banging meat-cleavers and marrow bones together to
produce 'rough music'. The butcher's apron conveys the usual sexual innuendo
– 'All upright members for ever'.

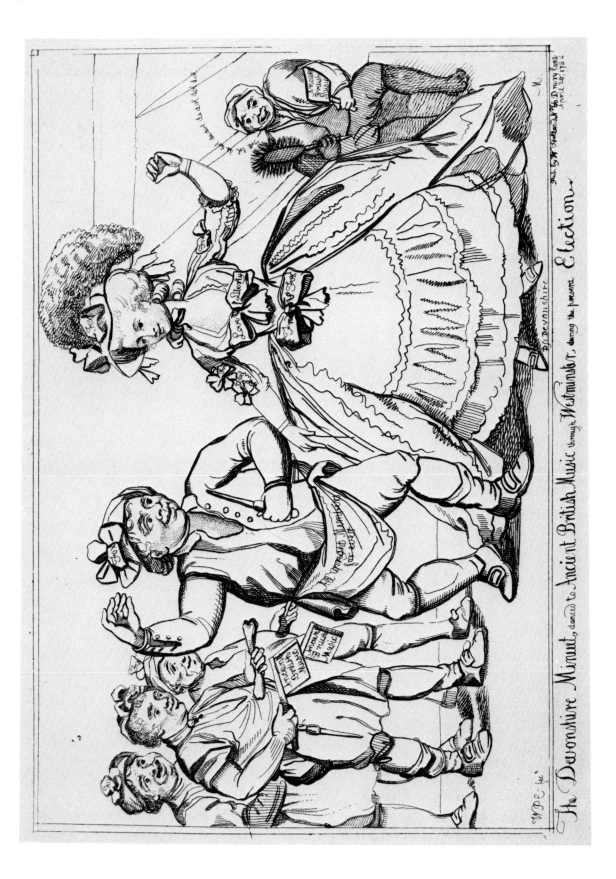

The Devonshire Minuet, danced to Ancient British Music through Westminster, during the present Election.

85. BMC 6493   3 April 1784   Collings
Female Influence; or the Devons---e Canvas
The very first satire on the Duchess's canvassing for Fox. Note the exposure of her legs, and the bribe being offered by her female companion on the right. The Duchess was deeply hurt by these prints and complained bitterly that she was no more active than several other women soliciting votes for Fox. She also claimed to have kissed almost no-one during the canvass.

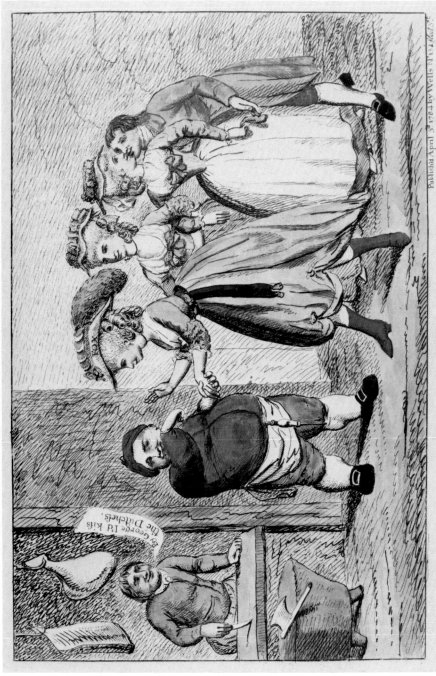

FEMALE INFLUENCE: or, the DEVONS^{hir}—E CANVAS.

By George I'd kiss the Dutchess.

Publish'd April 3 1784 by Wells N°132 Fleet St.

86. BMC 6494   3 April 1784   Rowlandson
The Patriotic Duchess's on their Canvass
The Duchess of Devonshire canvassing with the Duchess of Portland (rear left).
A less aggressive satire in that Rowlandson portrays the young butchers in an
extremely genteel fashion: they look more like young bucks or men about town
than like tradesmen.

THE TWO PATRIOTIC DUCHESS'S ON THEIR CANVASS. 8 ap. 1784

Requesting the favour of an early Poll.

Rowlandson

Ds. Portland   Dss. Devonshire

87. BMC 6533   April 1784
     A Certain Duchess kissing Old-Swelter-in-Grease the Butcher for his Vote
     The title of this print, together with the butcher wiping his lips, makes this print
     extraordinarily effective. Note the dog fouling the Duchess's dress, and the
     conspicuous meat cleaver, a reference to the slang term 'cleaver' meaning a
     woman of easy virtue. Probably one of the harshest prints on the Duchess of
     Devonshire.

A Certain Dutcheſs kiſsing

Old SWELTER-IN-GREASE *the Butcher for his Vote*

O' Times! O' Manners!

The Women Wear Breeches & the Men Petticoats

RAYFORD SCULP

12 Ap. 1784

88. BMC 5876   12 July 1781   Gillray?
Sir Samuel House
A somewhat more sedate portrayal of House attributed – somewhat doubtfully
– to Gillray. Note the punchbowl with the inscription 'Fox for Ever'. It was
common practice in eighteenth-century taverns to have punchbowls with such
toasts and inscriptions.

SIR SAMUEL HOUSE.

Libertas et natale Solum.

London Published Jul. 15. 1795 by C. Knight, Berwick Street.

89. BMC 6560   29 April 1784   Rowlandson?
The Tipling Dutchess Returning from Canvassing
Possibly by Rowlandson, though not so attributed in the British Museum
Catalogue. House acts as a link-boy for the Duchess who is portrayed as both
drunk and décolletée, leaning on the arm of Fox (to left) and another gentlemen
on the right.

90. BMC 5679   9 June 1780   Gillray
   No Popery or Newgate Reformer
   An attack on the Gordon Rioters. The print and its motto implies that the
   Protestant Association was a mere excuse for rioters to engage in pillage and
   rapine. Newgate Gaol burns in the background. The use of the term 'reformer'
   in the title, though clearly ironic, was unusual for the time.

NO POPERY or NEWGATE REFORMER.

Tho' He Says he's a Protestant,   look at the Print,
The Face and the Bludgeon, will give you a hint,
Religion he cries, in hopes to deceive,
While his practice is only to burn and to thieve.
Publish'd as the Act Directs, June 5.th 1780 by I. Catch of St Giles's.

91. BMC 9202   20 April 1798   Gillray
London Corresponding Society, alarm'd
The London Corresponding Society was the largest of the numerous artisan
radical societies established during the 1790s and advocated parliamentary and
social reform. Gillray turns their meeting into a vision of hell. The figures are
both grotesque and satanic, and the ascending stairs (rear right) convey the
sense that we are in the darkest depths. The cause of the radicals' anxiety was
the recent arrest of a number of their leaders.

London Corresponding Society, alarm'd, Vide. Guilty Conscience

92.   BMC 7867   23 May 1791   Gillray
The Rights of Man – or – Tommy Paine, the little American Taylor, taking the
Measure of the Crown, for a new pair of Revolution Breeches
Gillray's savage attack on the former tailor and exciseman, Tom Paine, the
author of the most important radical tract of the 1790s, *The Rights of Man*.
Note Paine's ragged appearance, and the French pig-tail.

"THE RIGHTS OF MAN;_ or TOMMY PAINE, the little American Taylor, taking the Measure of the CROWN, for a new Pair of Revolution-Breeches.

93. BMC 9228   12 June 1798   Gillray
United Irishmen upon Duty
This print refers to the bloody Irish rising of 1798. The United Irish, pro-French and usually Catholic, are depicted here as a fiendish band of murderers. The nightmare quality of the scene is enhanced by depicting the attack on the farmer and his wife as occurring at night.

United Irishmen upon Duty.

94. BMC 9229   13 June 1798   Gillray
United Irishmen in Training
A grotesque companion to Plate 93, showing the Irish rebels preparing for battle.

United Irishmen in Training.

95. BMC 7883   29 June 1791   Gillray
The National Assembly Petrified/The National Assembly Revivified
The print refers to Louis XVI and Marie Antoinette's flight to Varennes and
subsequent recapture. Gillray depicts his usual grotesque Jacobins as first
petrified and then exultant. Note the frogs threaded from the cook's waist in the
lower compartment on the left.

96. BMC 8114   24 July 1792   Dent
   A Limited Monarchy
   A vicious satire on the invasion of the Tuileries on 20 June 1792; the king is
   held at spearpoint by a grotesque group of Jacobins.

Sanction the Decrees!
No Veto!!!

Pub. by J. Aitken No 14

A LIMITED MONARCHY.
or, the NEGATIVE power of France
Surrounded by the patriotic Furies
of the 20. Ult.

97. BMC 9181   1 March 1798   Gillray
Consequences of a Successful French Invasion, no. 1 Plate 2nd
For this famous Gillray series see plate *61*. The scene is the House of Lords after an imaginary take-over by the French.

Consequences of a Suc—cessful French Invasion.

Sir John Dalrymple inv.

London. Pub.d March 1.st 1798 by J. Gillray, N.o 27 S.t James's Street. — Price 6.d — Colourd 1s/6.

J. Gillray fecit.

N.º I. — Plate 2.d — "We explain de Rights of Man to de Noblesse." — Scene. The House of Lords.

Description. — A Guillotine, which is placed on the Throne; the royal Chairs being removed, pour ac-commoder les Etrangers. (in English) To accommo-date the Strangers. Two Turkish-Mutes, with strongbow Bowstrings, each his Hand on his Mouth, stand as Sup-porters. The House empty of Peers. On a Board is written, "Solitudinem faciunt, Pacem appellant." (in En-glish) "They (that is the French) create Solitude, and call it Peace." The Cap of Liberty above the Canopy, below which is painted in capital Letters "Confusion to all Order". A French Admi-ral, looking at the Tapestry, which represents the Defeat of ye Spanish invincible Armada, & the Portraits of the Immortal English Commanders, says "Me like not de Omen, defray it; French Soldiers with Swords, Phis. K.s & naked Bayonets, attack the Tapestry, on one side of the Room. A Sea-Captain, on the Top of a Ladder, pours down ye Tapes-try from above; his Lieutenant sets fire to it below K at the same Time pulls the feet of the Ladder to break his Superior Neck, saying "This is an easier Way of getting Preferment than in English Way... Un Commandant en Chef, in English, The Commander in Chief, in lawful Republican Uniform, point-ing at the Mace, says "Here take away this Bauble - but if there be any Gold a-bout it, it could it to my Lodging "A French-Soldier carries it away on his Shoulder. The Bust of Pitt on the Table, in the Middle between those of Fox & Richlieu.

98. BMC 9182 1 March 1798
   Consequences of a Successful French Invasion, no. 3 Plate 2nd
   Gillray depicts the consequences for the common people of a French invasion:
   slavery imposed in the cause of liberty, garlic and *soup maigre* instead of
   English roast beef, and the overweening tyranny of the French order.

Consequences of a Successfull French Invasion.

No VIII. Plate 2d. — We teach de English Republicans to work. — Scene A Wheatfield.

99. BMC 8122   20 September 1792   Gillray
Un petit Souper, a la Parisienne; – or – a Family of Sans-Culotts refreshing
after the fatigues of the day
An extraordinarily powerful and self-explanatory attack on the September
Massacres in Paris in 1792.

Potion

Down la Gueule.

Vive le Epalée

Sauver la Grand

Propriété de la Nation.

Pub.^d Sepr 20.th 1792. by H. Humphrey N.º 18 Old Bond Street.

Un petit Souper, a la Parisienne. —— or —— A Family of Sans Culotts refreshing, after the fatigues of the day.

Epigram extempore on seeing the above Print.

On Maigre Days each, had his Dish
Of Soup, or Salad, Eggs, or Fish;
But now 'tis human Flesh they gnaw,
And ev'ry Day is Mardi Gras.

Here, as you see, and as 'tis known,
Frenchmen mere Cannibals are grown,

100. BMC 8624   2 March 1795   Gillray
Patriotic Regeneration – viz – Parliament Reform'd, a la Francoise – that is – Honest Men (i.e. Opposition) In the Seat of Justice
The imaginary impeachment of the younger Pitt, led by his old opponents – Fox (in the Speaker's chair), Stanhope (who reads the charges), Erskine, Sheridan, Grafton, Lauderdale and Derby. The benches of the House of Commons are crowded with grotesque demotic figures. The theme of this print is analogous to that of *The Consequences of a Successful French Invasion* series. Gillray also implies that there is an intimate connection between the parliamentary opposition and the radical and republican groups in London.

Pub. March 4th 1795 by H. Humphrey, Nº 37, New Bond Street.

Patriotic Regeneration. — viz. — Parliament Reform'd, a la Françoise. — that is. — Honest Men (i.e. Opposition) in the Seat of Justice

CHARGES.
1st. For opposing the Rights of Subjects to dethrone their King.
2d. For opposing the Popular Protest to annihilate Nobility...

101. BMC 3909   September 1762
The St-te Quack
An attack on Lord Bute, George III's favourite (in the centre of the stage), and
on his putative mistress, George III's mother, the Princess Dowager (portrayed
as the falling rope walker). Bute is satirised as a quack, a popular means of
attacking eighteenth-century politicians (see plate *10*). In the right foreground is
a sailor, identified by his trousers, kerchief and hat, who belabours a kilted Scot.

The State QUACK

Sept 1762

France   Scotland
P/s Wales.   Ld Bute.

Publish'd according to Act of Parliament. Price

102. BMC 8145   21 December 1792   Gillray
French Liberty. British Slavery
Gastronomic politics. Gillray contrasts the bitterly complaining but well-fed
Englishman (right) with the enthusiastic but emaciated Frenchman. The
contrast between garlic and snails, on the one hand, and roast beef and ale, on
the other, draws on a long-standing prejudice against the French diet and the
much-touted but exaggerated extent to which the English staple was supposed
to be beef.

FRENCH LIBERTY. BRITISH SLAVERY.

103. BMC 8288   3 January 1793   I. Cruikshank
French Happiness. English Misery
Cruikshank's version of the same subject as plate *102*. The Frenchmen are
rendered in a grotesque fashion, in the manner of Gillray, but the Englishmen,
though coarse-featured, have an altogether more realistic appearance.

104. BMC 2880   1747
The Beaux Disaster
The discomfort of an effete fop who has quarrelled with a butcher and ends up on a hook for his pains. The scene is the Strand with Temple Bar in the background.

The BEAUX DISASTER.

Ye Smarts, whose Merit lies in Dress,
Take warning by a Beaux Distress;
Whose Puppy Airs, & ill-turn'd Rage
Ventur'd with Butchers to engage.

But they wou'd Affronts to brook?
Have hung poor Fribble on a Hook.
While foul Disgrace, expos'd in Air,
The Butchers Shout & Ladies stare.

Satyr so strong, ye Tops, must strike you
How can you think, ye Fair, will like you,
Women of Sence in Men despise
The Antichs, they in Monkeys prize.

105. BMC 4476   1770   Adam Smith?
The Frenchman at Market
An example of the popular theme of the stalwart Englishman and the French
fop. Note the Frenchman's sufferings – a dog fouls his expensive stockings, a
sweep puts a mouse in his wig – even as the butcher strikes him to repay an
insult. Taking advantage of the altercation a Scot steals some meat from the
butcher's stall – this is a typical instance of the anti-Scottish sentiment that was
so frequently found in political cartoons in the first decade of George III's reign.

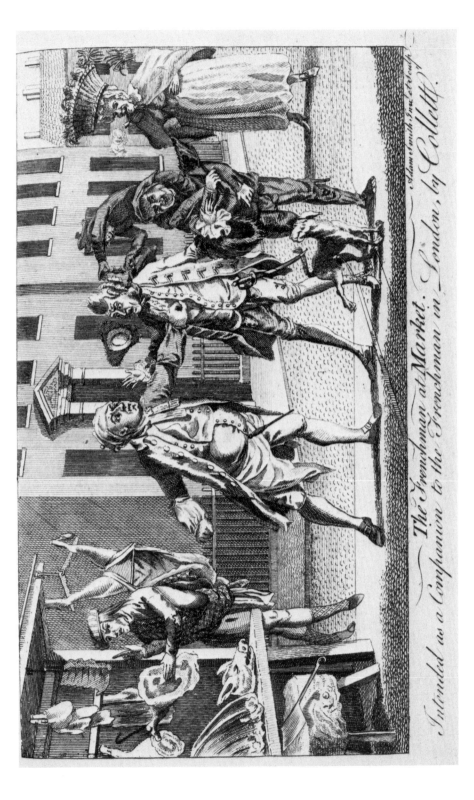

The Frenchman at Market. — London, by Collett.

Intended as a Companion to the Frenchman in London, by Collett.

Adam Smith Inv. et Sculp.

106. BMC 4477   10 November 1770   C. White
The Frenchman in London
Another patriotic confrontation. Note how much smaller the English butcher is than the Frenchman.

Jn.º Collet pinx.ᵗ   Le Francois a Londres.   C. White fecit

The FRENCHMAN in LONDON.

Printed for Robᵗ. Sayer Nº 53, in Fleet Street, & Jnº. Smith, Nº 35, in Cheapside.

Publiſhed as the Act directs Novᵗ 10, 1770.

107.   BMC 3904   September 1762
A Poor Man Loaded with Mischief. Or John Bull and his Sister Peg
Advertised as sold by John Williams (see plate *50*), the print attacks the Scots
and Lord Bute, the King's Scottish favourite. Bull is blind and horned – i.e.
cheated, a possible reference to the supposed affair between Bute and the
Princess Dowager. The print also attacks the peace negotiations with France of
1762.

Shoes and Boots made
or a New PEACE may be
Old Soles by Mack
from NORTH BRITON

D. Bedford   H Fox   John Bull, & Scotland.

SAWNEY MACKENSIE'S Compᵗˢ to ALL the SOUTHERNS
And, he hopes they will very soon comply
with the following
MODEST REQUEST

Each. Fat Lugged Loon. which dwell in this Town.
I beg ye'll give up your Dominions
And Gang to the North pass the River of Forth
And Feed upon Crowdy and Onions

It will do muckle qued to sweeten your blood
And make ye All, light as a feather.
Give your feeling a twitch when ye've pick'd up the Tick
By Ligging in Beds made of Heather.

In History we're told. King Jamie of Old.
(To his Reason who dare to object?)
To scratch Day and Night took Muckle delight
And swore 'twas too qued for a Subject.

Yet we promise the thing which so pleasur'd our King.
So, gang from your Wives, and your Daughters.
For Our Laddies in Town. must make All their own.
So prithe Gang soon to New Quarters.

Publish According to Act of Parliament
Sepᵗ 1762 P 6

Sept. 1762

108. BMC 5081   25 June 1772   Brandoine
France. England
French poverty and English prosperity in gastronomic form – cf. plates *102,
103*. Note the stalwart and cheeful demeanour of the English cook.

ENGLAND.

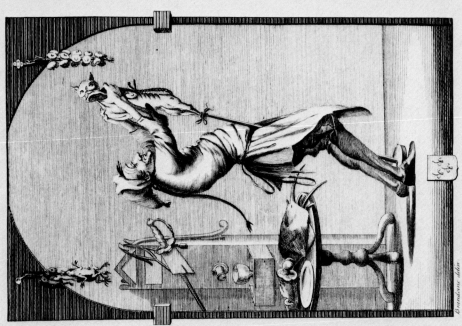

FRANCE.

Published by C. Bowles, No 25, Ludgate Hill, 25 June 1773.

Brandoin delin

109. BMC 5612   1779?   Gillray
   Politeness
   An early version of Gillray's Bull. Note particularly how the Bull figure is much more pugnacious and self-assured than the representation of him in the 1790s.

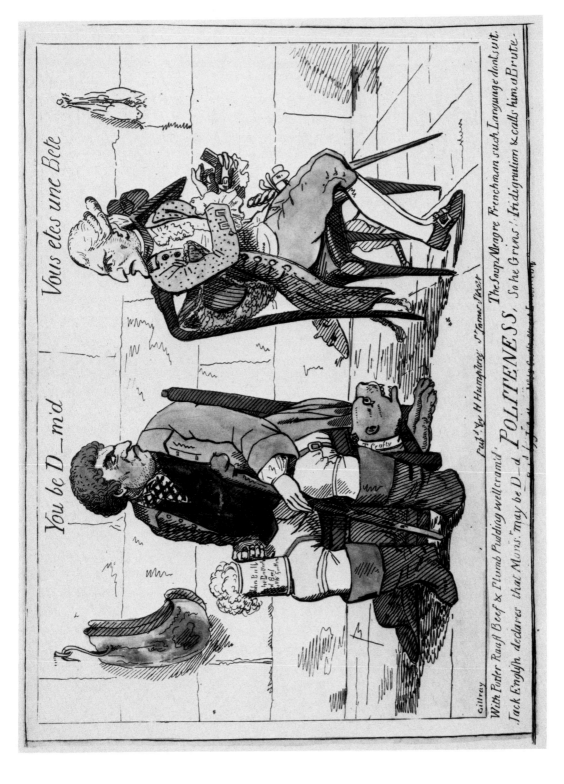

You be D__m'd   Vous etes une Bete

Gillray   Pub.d by H Humphrey. S.t James's Street

With Porter Rough Beef & Plumb Pudding well cram'd.   The Soup Maigre Frenchman such Language don't suit.
Jack English declares that Muns.r may be D__d.   So he Grins. & Indignation & calls him. a Brute.

POLITENESS,

110. BMC 9188   19 March 1798   Rd. Newton
'Treason!!'
An uncharacteristic Bull of the 1790s overtly defying the King, whose image is
papered to the wall.

111. BMC 9257   24 October 1798   Gillray
John Bull taking a Luncheon: – or – British Cooks cramming Old Grumble-Gizzard with Bonne Chere
British Admirals feed Bull with the French fleet. One of several celebrations of Nelson's victory at the Battle of the Nile. Even in this celebratory print Gillray does not depict Bull favourably.

JOHN BULL, taking a Luncheon: – or – British Cooks, cramming Old Grumble-Gizzard, with Bonne-Chère.

112. BMC 9237   16 July 1798   I. Cruikshank
Billy's Fantoccini or John Bull over Curious
A satire on the exclusion of strangers from the House of Commons during the Irish debates of 1798. The Fantoccini or marionette show, operated by puppet-master Pitt is a representation of the interior of the House of Commons. It is concealed from the view of Bull, who is portrayed as a yokel.

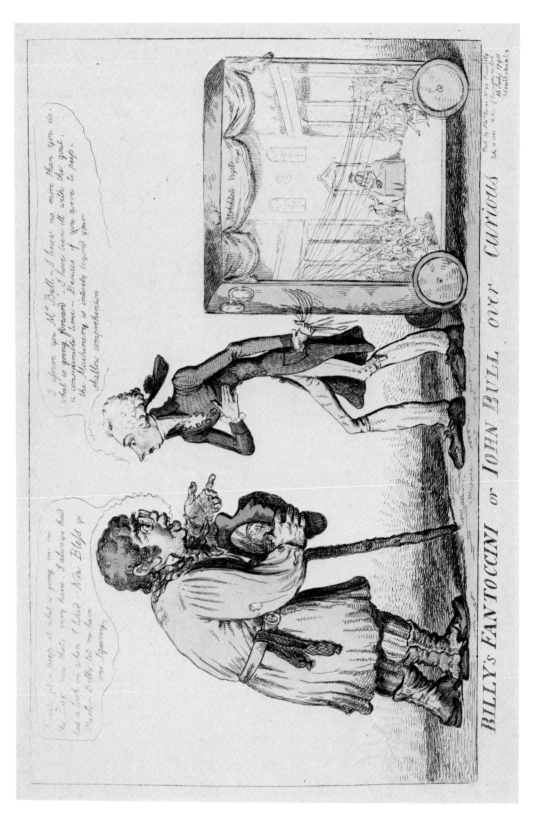

BILLY's FANTOCCINI or JOHN BULL over CURIOUS

113. BMC 9366   27 March 1799   Ansell?
A Week's Amusement for John Bull
A thin, refined Pitt and a vulgar, head-scratching Bull. A satire on the intense
interest in a horserace between Diamond and Hambletonian, even at a time of
national crisis, when more serious issues should have occupied the public.

There Master John,
we'll endeavour to furnish you
with a fresh Bill of fare next week.

Dang it Master — let times go how they will —
I must have a bet on one of them Horses.

Hamburgh Mails.
News from Paris.
German Gazzettes.
Report
of Secret Committe
Income Tax.
Race
between
Diamond &
Hambletonian;
at
New-market.
Deliverance of Europe.
News from Egypt.
ditto,
from Ireland.
Important
Intelligence
from
The East Indies.

A WEEKS AMUSEMENT for JOHN BULL.

Pub March 17 1799 by S.W. Fores 50 Piccadilly.

Books of Caricatures lent out for the Evening
19 March 1799
Ansell

114. BMC 8289 8 January 1793 Rowlandson
      Reform Advised/Reform Begun/Reform Compleat
      An attack on reform. The print shows the consequences of any change, namely
      the humiliation and eventual savaging of John Bull. Bull suffers a rapid and
      almost total deterioration as reform advances.

115. BMC 8328   3 June 1793   Gillray
John Bull's Progress
The misfortunes of war. Contented Bull fights for his country; his family falls into debt; and he returns home a cripple. The classic exposition of John Bull as impotent victim.

JOHN BULL going to the WARS.

JOHN BULL'S glorious Return.

JOHN BULL Happy.

JOHN BULL'S Property in danger.

JOHN BULL'S PROGRESS.

116. BMC 8703   13 December 1795   West?
Talk of an Ostrich! an Ostrich is nothing to him; Johnny Bull will swallow any thing
Bull forced to swallow the Seditious Meetings and Treasonable Practices Bills (or so called Convention Bills) of 1795. Bull is bloated – implying that he has had to swallow much in the past. The print is extraordinarily visually effective. The two bills restricted public meetings and created the offence of constructive treason. Both bills were aimed at stopping the activities of the radical societies.

What it sticks in your Throat does it? Oh
I'll ram it down I warrant you, and when it is once
past, you'll easily digest it: you must not be
Obstinate Johnny, when Laws are made you have
nothing to do but to Obey them!!!

Talk of an OSTRICH! an OSTRICH is nothing to him, Johnny Bull will swallow any thing!!

117.   BMC 8710   1795?   T. French
A Freeborn Englishman
A strongly anti-government print, showing a truly miserable and shackled
Englishman. One of the several attacks on the punitive legislation of 1795 (cf.
116, 118, 119).

T.French.

A FREEBORN ENGLISHMAN,

the Admiration of the World; the Envy of Surrounding Nations;
&c &c.

118. BMC 8711   1795

A Free Born Englishman!

A general attack on the government, clearly referring to the Two Acts but also to the high levels of taxation (necessary to sustain the war against the French) and to increased poverty, symbolised by the debtors' prison in the right background of the print.

A FREE BORN ENGLISHMAN!
THE ADMIRATION of the WORLD !!!
AND THE ENVY of SURROUNDING NATIONS !!!!!

119. BMC 8693   23 November 1795   West
A Lock'd Jaw for John Bull
Bull here is shown as a citizen rather than a farmer. The technique is somewhat like that in plate *116* by the same artist. The technique in both prints is what Gombrich has called 'anomalous juxtaposition', and it is that that explains much of the print's visual effect.

A LOCK'D JAW for JOHN BULL

FURTHER READING

BOOKS

David Alexander and Richard T. Godfrey, *Painters and Engraving: The Reproductive Print from Hogarth to Wilkie* (Yale Center for British Art, New Haven, Conn., 1980).

John Barrell, *The Dark Side of the Landscape: The Rural Poor in English Painting 1730–1840* (Cambridge, 1980).

David Erdman, *Blake: Prophet Against Empire* (Princeton, N.J., 1954).

M. D. George, *English Political Caricature: A Study in Opinion and Propaganda* (2 vols., Oxford, 1959).

M. D. George, *Hogarth to Cruikshank: Social Change in Graphic Satire* (London, 1967).

Douglas Hay, Peter Linebaugh and E. P. Thompson (eds.), *Albion's Fatal Tree* (London, 1975).

Sir Ambrose Heal, *London Tradesmen's Cards in the XVIIIth Century, An Account of their Origin and Use* (London, 1925).

Draper Hill, *Mr. Gillray, Caricaturist* (London, 1965).

Ronald Paulson, *Emblem and Expression: Meaning in English Art of the Eighteenth Century* (Cambridge, Mass., 1975).

Ronald Paulson, *Hogarth: His Life, Art and Times* (2 vols., London, 1971).

Robert Raines, *Marcellus Laroon* (London, 1966).

W. Roberts, *The Cries of London* (London, 1924).

E. P. Thompson, *The Making of the English Working Class* (London, 1965).

ARTICLES

Herbert M. Atherton, 'The Mob in Eighteenth-Century Caricature', *Eighteenth-Century Studies* 12, 1 (1978).

John Brewer, 'Theater and Counter-Theater in Georgian Politics: The Mock Elections at Garrat', *Radical History Review* 22 (1979–80).

E. H. Gombrich, 'The Cartoonist's Armory', *Meditations on a Hobby Horse* (3rd ed., London, 1978).

Ronald Paulson, 'Burke's Sublime and the Representation of Revolution', *Culture and Politics from Puritanism to the Enlightenment*, ed. Perez Zagorin (London, 1980).

Charles Press, 'The Georgian Political Print and Democratic Institutions', *Comparative Studies in Society and History* 19 (1977).

Alaisdair Smart, 'Dramatic Gesture and Expression in the Age of Hogarth and Reynolds', *Apollo* 82 (1965).

E. P. Thompson, 'Patrician Society, Plebeian Culture', *Journal of Social History* 7 (1974).

E. P. Thompson, 'Eighteenth-Century English Society: class struggle without class?', *Social History* 3 (1978).